BUCK PETERSON'S

COMPLETE GUIDE TO
FISHING

BY

BUCK "BUCK" PETERSON

ILLUSTRATIONS BY

J. ANGUS "SOURDOUGH" MCLEAN

D1446182

TEN SPEED PRESS
Berkeley | Toronto

Information contained in this guidebook is a collection of facts and fancies gathered over many minutes of Buck's long and varied life as a master guide. If, in the active use of this information, someone gets snagged, Buck apologizes to the next of kin and is off the hook. Also, Buck's blueblood family background extends far back into royal Norwegian history, and he is entitled by fiat to highlight the genetic failings of lesser Scandinavians, particularly the Swedish.

Ten Speed Press
PO Box 7123
Berkeley, California 94707

Cover Design by Betsy Stromberg
Interior design by Headcase Design, Philadelphia, PA
Illustrations by J. Angus "Sourdough" McLean

The Library of Congress has cataloged the first edition as follows:
Peterson, B.R.
    [Complete Guide to Fishing]
    Buck Peterson's complete guide to fish/B.R. "Buck" Peterson; illustrations by J. Angus "Sourdough" McLean.
    p. cm.
    ISBN 1-58008-736-1
1. Fishing—Minnesota—Humor. 2. Fishing—Minnesota—Caricatures and cartoons. 3. Fishes, Fresh-water—Humor. I. Title.
PN6231.F5P4 1991
818'.5402—dc20
                    90-20837

The publisher certifies that this book was actually written by Buck and not cribbed from other fishing guidebooks, though there were times when the latter seemed the better idea.

Printed in the United States of America

First printed in 1991
1 2 3 4 5—10 09 08 07 06

The publisher and author would like to apologize for the errors that appear in the following pages. None of these are their fault and the printer gets off clean as well. The guilty will be hunted down like dogs and punished in the leatherbound edition.

Page 23: Delete "Catching fish isn't important. Just being there is."
Page 62: Fish sticks are NOT supposed to have scales.
Page 90: Ocean fish pulled from oil spills need less cooking oil.
Page 106: Under outdoors, hygiene, line 8: Add "A waste is a terrible thing to mind."
Page 118: Buck's Bonus Tip for Swedish Ice-fishermen: Fishing on ice-skating rinks can be very productive.
Page 131: Wearing hemp underwear will not get you high.
Page 146: Under post-bass tournament party, line 6, insert: "Don't fire until you see the whites of her thighs."
Page 147: Trouser trout spawn year-round.
Page 153: The medical use of marijuana for fishing related illnesses is legal in Oregon.
Page 160: Lipstick on the collar can be removed with a good commercial stain-remover.
Page 165: Drinking like a fish is the first step in a 12 step big-mouth program.
Page 171: Line 8: Add "Small breasted women have feelings too."
Page 172: Monkfish are the preferred Friday lunch entrée at the abbey.
Page 180: Under Tips: Add "If you give a cat a fish, it eats for a day. If you give a cat to a coyote, you can charge admission."

DEDICATION

This newly polished edition is newly dedicated to
two fine gentlemen who willingly took a grateful
young lad fishing. Uncle Tony Peterson, the best
walleye fisherman on Little Pine Lake, illuminated
the inherent goofiness of fishing by showing Buck
how to catch big fish trolling backwards out of a
Lund aluminum boat. And Buck's older brother,
Dave, taught him how to catch garbage cans full
of crappies out of a seventeen-foot square stern
Herter's canoe on Red Rock Lake. Their generosity
cannot be underestimated.

CONTENTS

INTRODUCTION

Like all consumer sports, fishing has become more complicated. As a public service, Buck comes to the rescue with a collector's edition of fishing rod and real tips. He agreed to write this book on the condition he was allowed to reveal the naked truth about fishing. In this spirit, Buck wrote most of this book while naked.

Buck realizes that fathers are often absent in homes and women, genetically engineered to only clean fish, simply cannot pass on the lore of yesteryear. For many fly fishermen, only yesterday was 1956. This guide speaks of fishing's unspoken importance for modern man—the necessity of getting away from the high-pitched needs of the modern woman.

Like *Buck Peterson's Complete Guide To Deer Hunting*, this inexpensive paperback is a required textbook in Buck's Wilderness School and Famous Sportsman Correspondence Course, and is not just another cash cow for the author.

THE MOST FREQUENTLY ASKED QUESTIONS ABOUT FISH AND FISHING

1. *I like to dress my fish properly. What do you suggest?*
   Never wear white after Labor Day.
2. *How do you pronounce "crappie"? Some make it sound like the super-sized crap you take after a super-sized fishwich "meal" at a local fast-food joint.*
   Cunnilinguists who study things oral break the word into two pieces— "craw" (as in in-laws that stick in your craw) and pee (as in the yellow snow water used to flavor Canadian beer).

3. *My doctor says I should eat more fish to get Omega-3 into my system but I can't seem to catch any more fish.*
   The more expensive cat food has the best fish.

4. *How do you keep your worm wet?*
   I'll answer that question off the air.

5. *Why do fish seek deeper water in the summer?*
   To escape the surface fire from the party boats.

6. *What's the difference between a shitload and a boatload of crappies?*
   The boat.

7. *Fish oil pills make my breath smell like my wife's bicycle seat. What should I do?*
   Gargle with a mixture of water and vinegar.

8. *How will I know when it is too cold to ice fish?*
   After the honeymoon, it's never too cold to ice fish.

9. *Is fly-fishing normal? Is it something genetic or caused by social pressure?*
   Researchers say that a reduced immune system is the real culprit.

10. *Can small children be used as shark bait?*
    Only when school is out.

11. *I am a barista, not a coffee clerk. Baristas have to remember a lot of stuff and are prohibited from taking recreational drugs while operating the espresso machine.*
    One large cup of Folgers to go, please.

12. *The new Japanese outboards don't pollute the air or water. Does Honda make a horse?*
    If not now, soon. With more horsepower and less gaseous emissions.

13. *I want to spend a couple weeks observing you in your habitat to finish my study of lower primates. What month works best for you?*
    Don't be such a chump.

FISH

WHAT IS A FISH?

In Webster's view, it doesn't take much to be a fish—just be any one of the three classes of cold-bloods living in water and have permanent gills for breathing, fins, and, to be a "real" fish, scales. The jawless fish family has only two American members, the hagfish and lamprey. The weak backboned cartilaginous family includes sharks and rays. The bony fish family contains many of our finned friends and the subject of this book.

Outside of ichthyologists, Buck wants you to know that the entire fish group is receiving a bum rap. The trouble is indicated in our language. If you drink like a fish, you shouldn't (unless you are having dinner with the in-laws). If something is fishy, it's highly suspect. A fish story is a fable fabricated while you pull up the driveway with lipstick on your collar. Corporate career women are unfairly described as barracudas (especially since there is a much wider range of predators to choose from). Red herrings are false clues in a good mystery. Wrapped up in a newspaper, a dead mackerel is an important part of Italian communications.

The animal world understands the importance of fish. There isn't a dog of good breeding alive that doesn't want to roll on the ground on top of a decaying carp carcass. Show Buck a cat that doesn't prefer a fresh slab of fish flesh over canned commercial mush. Seagulls need fish to reload their bomb bays. Grizzlies love to chomp on big salmon, and nature societies love to put the bite on the wealthy for those photo opportunities.

This paean to fish could go on forever, but there are other fish to fry.

OUTSIDE PARTS OF A FISH

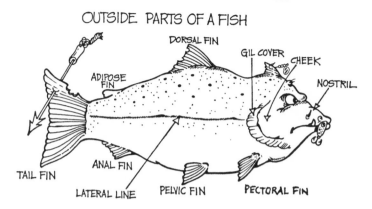

WHAT A FISH LOOKS LIKE

(Editor's note: The following material may seem elementary, but many will admit it really is.) All fish have common characteristics, with freshwater fish varying only slightly from saltwater fish. The principal differences are between what you see on the outside and the horrors within.

FINS: The tail or caudal fin is used for propulsion and steering. When a fish is being retrieved, the tail fin is used as a drag. The anal fin is named after its strategic location near the "back door" and is used to wave away embarrassing gas bubbles. The pelvic fin props a fish at rest on the bottom and is used by slower fish to wave on passing predator fish. Fish pass one another only on the left (port) side. The pectoral fin when waved invites friendly social intercourse. The dorsal fins are what sharks use to give fear to bathers. The forward spiny fin is used to impale troublesome neighbors and the trailing soft fin assists locomotion. The adipose fin is an indication of the inbreeding endemic to hatchery fish, similar to the vestigial tails on European royalty and certain American political family dynasties.

GILL COVER: Where gills are stored for safekeeping.

OTHER OUTSIDE BODY PARTS: Includes nostrils, cheeks, and lips, which are covered in great detail elsewhere.

INSIDE PARTS OF A FISH

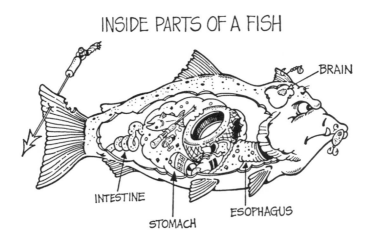

INSIDE PARTS: The fish brain is located high in the cranial cavity and seldom used. Fish psychologists have tried to monitor fish brain waves for any evidence of species identity and self-esteem. Unfortunately for fish rights activists, the brain waves indicate only a slavish weakness for easy food.

The guts of the matter focus on the passages—from the mouth, through the esophagus, temporary residence in the stomach, and power flushing via the internal sewer pipe. A full stomach of garbage will conceal organs pushed out of their traditional hiding spots: the heart, home of all romantic fish notions and broken only when a fly fisherman forgets the French kiss before release; the liver, an overworked poison fighter; the kidneys, pushing water into water; the gas bladder, for setting the proper depth levels; and the over-sized sex organs, which are too embarrassing to be included in a guidebook read by the whole family.

SENSE

HEARING: Fish have inner ears that isolate and identify sounds. These inner ears are found inside the skull, one each behind the eyes, and contain three semicircular canals and three ear stones that rattle about the not-quite-full cranial cavity. The stones are covered by sensory hair cells, and sound waves move tiny bones called otoliths to stimulate the hair cells which send complicated messages to a brain preoccupied with your awful smell upstream.

Researchers estimate that fish can hear sound waves in about twice the range heard by a fisherman listening closely to his wife. With water five times more dense than air, sound travels about five times faster. This should not stop you from telling your mate to shut his/her piehole.

SIGHT: Few fish are as blind as the batfish and most have good eyesight. Evolution has played a large part in the particulars of eye placement. For example, the two eyes on the same side of a halibut or flounder resulted from constant irritation to the downside eye of these bottom feeders. Somewhere along the evolutionary trail, the bottom eye was persuaded to join its buddy topside. Fish ophthalmologists complain that since the top eye doesn't have to work so hard, signs of "lazy eye" have appeared and crossed eyes are reported. Predictably, older flat fish often complain about blurry vision while swimming in the dark.

The fish eye sits in a hard socket with a filmlike covering. Without a discernable lid, it's impossible to tell what they might be doing or thinking. They may be just playing dead. If they are, start filleting.

Of supreme importance to the lure industry, fish are not color-blind. In clear, bright water, bass recognize the season's flashiest colors, while others with more sensitive peepers (like walleyes) can only distinguish particular colors. Water filters out color the deeper you go, making brightness and movement more important. How far fish can see depends on the clarity of the water, with an average between fifteen and twenty-five feet. Predators enjoy superior eyesight and three square meals a day.

Fish can see sportsmen standing along the edge of a riverbank. If you have to get closer, crouch or crawl carefully and wear a gillie suit. It's one of the rare occasions in life when it pays to be short.

If you are saltwater fishing, the fish jump out of the water to try to get a good look at the big fish on the other end of the line. The biggest game fish tend to be a little farsighted and it won't be until you lean over the side of the boat for a gaffing that the fish will get a better look at you and, no doubt, experience major embarrassment.

If a fish does see you, your fishing day isn't necessarily over. Young fish have short memories and the oldest fish even forget why they're in the water in the first place.

TASTE: While we humans only have taste buds in our mouths, fish can have them most anywhere. Catfish, for example, have taste buds in their whiskers, fins, and mouth as well as on their pretty lips. When a cell of a bud senses a chemical substance, a message goes to their tiny brains to be interpreted as good to eat or not. Fish mouth a lure or bait to taste it and that leads to many an innocent downfall.

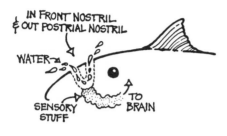

IN FRONT NOSTRIL
& OUT POSTRIAL NOSTRIL
WATER
SENSORY STUFF
TO BRAIN

SMELL: Fish olfactory organs are in much the same place as yours, below the eyes and above the mouth. Their nostrils (or naves) lead to cavities filled with sensory nerves that are connected to the brain. Some fish have folds (or lamellae) that greatly increase the surface and acuity of their snouts.

Early salmon studies show fish are repelled by human scent; first by the smell of Norwegian commercial fishermen, second by the smell of the cannery worker who stuffed them into a ten-pound can, and third the Catholics who created the demand. It was shown at the time that fish also avoided smells of bear paws, sea lions, and cracker crumb breading.

Each fish species has its distinctive odor, and smell helps a fish locate its own school, identify bait-fish for food, or alert it to a predator. Threatened or injured fish release cold sweat substances. Scientists theorize that each species releases chemicals to cause specific reactions—courting, spawning, and social order. Female fish exude "perfume" to start recreational foreplay. There is no concrete evidence that gastric distress can create methane buildup in the lower intestines of fish, but this theory may help explain why some fish always swim alone.

THE LATERAL LINE: This fish sense falls somewhere between feeling and hearing, and is a row of sensory organs that run roughly midway along the side of a fish and are sensitive to vibrations and pressure waves. On most fish, the line is easy to identify as it is darker than the rest of the fish. On others, just trust Buck—it's there.

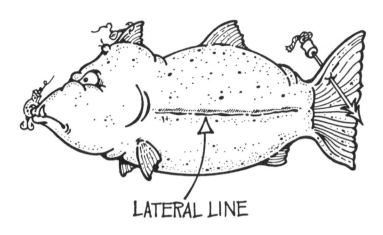

LATERAL LINE

The lateral line serves as an early warning to detect predators or a food source. It's further speculated that as fish movements create and measure vibrations against stationary objects using these organs, they are able to become masters of their habitat. It's not known if they can roll over on their side to mark the party boats hanging above them in the water.

FISH SEX AND SEXUALITY

There are two major fish sexes, male and female. Much like fly fishermen, a few fish species start off as one sex (usually male) and mature into the opposite sex. The catch and release process of an "outing" may accelerate this changeover. Several species and isolated individuals are hermaphroditic, and the distracting inner conflicts make these fish easy to catch.

Quite often, a fish must be opened up to identify the sex. Male fish have gonads hanging between the swim bladder and digestive tubes in the dorsal part of the body. The sperm duct exits with the urethra behind the anus. Very few male fish have a johnson.

The female produces eggs in ovaries situated in a similar location and releases them through an oviduct shortly before spawning. For most fish, fertilization takes place outside the body and creates an emotional distance between the sexes that cannot be closed without therapy.

Some fish, such as sharks and rays, are live-bearers with eggs carried and hatched within the mother. These tasty fry are released when Dad is out of town.

In a few fish, the males can be distinguished from the females without cutting them open. For example, colors of the male trout during the spawn intensify and brighten. During the spawn, male salmon develop a well-defined hook in the jaw and often a dorsal hump. (P.S. A "dorsal hump" is not an activity.) A more dramatic difference between the sexes in saltwater fish is found in the dolphin. The male head is square, which suggests Swedish genetic background, while the female head is round, except where she has taken her normal domestic lumps.

It's not known precisely what stimulates reproduction, but scientists suggest changes in water temperature and light. For understandable reasons, too much light slows or stops the amour. During reproduction, fins position the two consenting adult fish and a single bump is sufficient for both the sperm and eggs to be released and fertilized on the run. Even in these modern times, there is no interest in recreational sex and that is attributed to the lack of teeth brighteners in today's fluoridated waters.

AGE

Most fish don't live long enough to swim in Golden Pond, what with pollution, depth finders, type A tournament fishermen, and all the gewgaw tackle and techniques described in trade magazines. If a fish could go full-term, the process would look like this:

BABY FISH

Spits up lures and worms, and has untrained bowel habits.

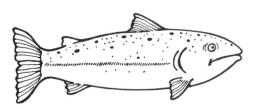

ADOLESCENT FISH

Threatens to leave home and rent its own habitat; appearance marked by pimplelike growths around face and upper back.

ADULT FISH

Belongs to species support groups and notices a certain amount of humdrum in its life. Fearful of the spawn.

FISH SENIORS

Like old fishermen, old fish die and often smell that way long before the event. Old fish skin tissue breaks down and arthritis makes it difficult to move the fins. Eyes and cheeks sink, and the skin gets leathery. A heavy lure can pull teeth out. A mild form of Alzheimer's disease can occur and that period is most dangerous to the trophy old timer. If the case is severe, the fish will see the lure but won't remember what to do with it. When fish die, some sink, some will be eaten, but most will rise up and float over to your part of the beach.

HOW TO JUDGE AGE: Not all large fish are older fish. Size depends on food, habitat, predators, and genetic commands of the species. Unlike most mammals, fish can grow after maturity. Much like your mother-in-law. If the right foods are available, fish can continue growing all their adult lives, so much so that a colony of retired film critics are petitioning the Florida legislature to declare Liz Taylor the state fish.

✔ *THE OFFICIAL WAY TO JUDGE AGE:* Catch lots of fish and assign years by grouping according to length. If you know where the fish were stocked or tagged, just read the date on the tag.

✔ *THE BEST WAY:* Fish in the wild grow slower in the winter and this slowing shows up as concentric rings on bony structure such as vertebrae, scales, and inner ear bones (otoliths). For example, the sagittal otoliths of young walleyes can be read as one ring per day. The older ones grow by season. An exception to this count is a fish living year-round in an unnatural habitat, such as a heated discharge pool.

Oceangoing fish that migrate to stay in warm water don't show age easily so the dorsal spines are measured. An important general rule to remember: Like mammals, females grow at a faster rate than males, not so much in length but in weight, especially around the middle. Female fish also develop spindly looking fins, and, if not caught at their sexual peak, may experience hot flashes, night sweats, and incontinence. This in turn will lead to irritability, insomnia, depression, and mood swings. Male fish age gracefully and swim quietly into the night, marked with thought lines forward of the gill cover and a more distinguished silver coloring of the scales.

WHAT THEY EAT

To the naked eye, fish exhibit two drives, fear or hunger. Common to all matriarchal societies, Mom Nature supports the survival of the fittest and allows the large to eat the small. Larger fish eat their young or smaller species, which in turn eat zooplankton out of frustration. Rough fish are eaten by those who don't know any better. Trout often go to bed hungry, half full of skinny insects and dry flies. Timid hatchery fish take a minnow only if they know it's dead.

Fish that eat their own feel no social stigma and usually start with those youngsters who have not been paying attention at fish school. When the family is not available, fish-eaters look for any new kids on the block. Up-and-coming predators will be taken next. Only then will most fish look elsewhere, such as under your boat.

The largest and oldest fish eat first. Adult fish will not forage meals for their young. Smaller fish eat only after the larger fish have filled up, burped once, and moved on. One predictable twist of artificial nature is that hatchery fish leave for the sea too early, providing a windfall for predators waiting at the ocean's gate.

All fish have a preferred diet, but favorite foods are often available for only a short time. Young fish experiment with different foods and throw up if it doesn't taste good. Predators, on the other hand, will concentrate on easy-to-swallow fish. A typical pattern is to sneak up and inhale the little, softer fish from behind and, until the digestive juices start working, it's just a couple of fish swimming along, having a good time. If the fish swallows the smaller fish headfirst, the little fish has one chance to swim through and out the bung of the larger fish. This maneuver really irritates the larger predator, especially if the little predator grabs an intestinal snack on the way out.

If they came from a large family, fish tend to eat too fast and too often. If they came from smaller, more affluent trout families, table manners prevail, and they take their time, chewing their food carefully and thankfully. Fish with underdeveloped taste buds don't care what food is—only where it might be.

The single documented case of a fish leaving its habitat to eat is from the log-book of Buck's Lunker Bass Resort where a monster bullhead crawled up out of Big Babe Lake and ate out of an unattended picnic basket.

A DAY IN THE LIFE OF A FISH

BEFORE 8 A.M.: Early mornings during sport fishing season are a time for troubled sleep, quick energy snacks, and last minute strategy sessions with the school. Bass count the multicolored lures stuck in the sunken tree stumps, and muskies spit out the hooks swallowed during the night.

	WILD FISH	*CATCH AND RELEASE FISH* *(OR HATCHERY FISH)*
8 A.M.	Open eyes	Open one eye
9 A.M.	Fight predators	Dorsal fin exercises
10 A.M.	Cruise territory looking for chicks	Eat abundant hatch without breaking water surface
11 A.M.	Spit out one hook	Lateral line flexes
NOON	Eat smaller predator	Have colors done
1 P.M.	Break mono line	Float to surface

2 P.M.	Cruise for more chicks	Let fly fisherman catch in net
3 P.M.	Fight predators	Photo sessions with fly fishermen
4 P.M.	Eat crustaceans	Slow recovery period
5 P.M.	Take dump	Quiet time
6 P.M.	Spit out last lure	More quiet time
7 P.M.	Roughhouse with pals	Still more quiet tim

AFTER 8 P.M.: Native fish enjoy a full day of sunlight and curse the darkness marked by the end of daylight saving time. Catch and release fish prefer fewer daylight hours as it really is too much stress being handled by even the most sensitive of fly fishermen. Wild fish continue to handle or ride rough harness on their basest biological needs: eating, making love, cruising the neighborhood, and keeping bullies and predators on the other side of the weed beds.

SCHOOLS

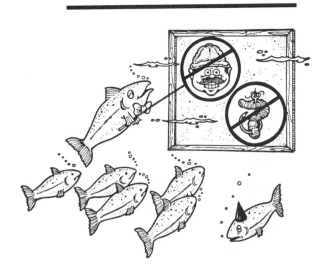

While some species do not school, most fish, whether large or smaller, whether for a day or for a lifetime, gather in groups to "school" around. Larger schools are found in metropolitan areas. In rural areas, class/teacher ratios are much smaller and the instruction is better received.

A large school of fish can shop for food over a wider area and, if food is found, communicate the whereabouts quicker. If a member of the school finds food and doesn't report it, he or she will be called in front of the principal predator and eaten if it's a second offense.

Single predators find it hard to bite on a tight school of twisting and turning baitfish and are easily confused by the frenzied activity. Predators themselves school and work a group of baitfish much like coyotes circling a sheep herd, dashing in for a quick snack.

Parents rely more on the schools to pass on cultural and societal values. Privately they will admit the babysitting function is a side benefit. Instructor fish pass on all social behavior in the schooling process through demonstrations and field trips. All young fish must have the permission of their parents, including a waiver of responsibility to take part in field trips. Prior to opening day, immature fish are shown where to hide in the weeds, under the dock, and under your boat. Instruction includes a lesson on the historical development of the artificial lure and how to recognize a catch and release fisherman by the cut of his waders.

MIGRATIONS

Migrations are either active or passive. The three generally agreed upon reasons for migration are alimental—for food; climatic—for preferred habitat, following the warmer waters; and gametic—to reproduce.

Fishermen are more familiar with the gametic motivations, and these spawning fish fall into two categories:

✔ *ANADROMOUS*: Moving from salt water to fresh-water to reproduce (like salmon, steelhead, and shad).

✔ *CATADROMOUS*: Moving from fresh water to salt-water (like eels).

GREAT MIGRATING FISH:

✔ *SALMON:* The five Pacific salmon originate in freshwater rivers or in hatcheries. If wild, salmon pair up and mate in clear streams, with the female digging a nest and depositing three to five thousand eggs. The male fertilizes the eggs and sweeps gravel over them. Then both parents die. This spares them parenting heartbreaks. The eggs hatch and the young fish stay in fresh-water up to eighteen months before going to sea for adventure. Once at sea, they swim for two to five years in the North Pacific, dodging Japanese drift nets and swim in a general counterclockwise direction unless it's daylight saving time. Roughly 5 percent survive the ocean to return home. Each original pair produces about ten fish that survive, eight of which are caught by fishermen and two of which are left to start all over again. When their biological clock alarm sounds, they return to reenact the parental saga of meeting, mating, and dying. Hatchery fish that accidentally end up in the wild spread general alarm about this genetic death wish and petition the wild stock to avoid the tradition and move with them to Canada.

In a cruel twist by Mom Nature, male salmon experience a change of life during the final spawning run, hooking their noses and turning shades of red, looking much like a bass fisherman talking with his wife about her "plumbing." The head and tail of a sockeye male turn green, scales and hairline recede, and a hump mysteriously rises on his back. All this makes him more attractive and fly fisherman switch to dry humpies with a weighted treble hook.

Improperly trained hatchery salmon keep bumping into the coastline until they find a river to climb. For both the wild and hatchery fish, man has erected an incredible barricade of obstacles to prevent continuation of the species. In addition to dams, manmade pollution confuses the fish that have been out to sea, and they are often unable to find their original rivers. While they sniff the shoreline for the lost homeland, unscrupulous U.S. Department of Natural Resources managers open a commercial season to lower supermarket prices.

Atlantic salmon may survive to migrate and spawn two or three times. Research conducted by the Underwater Deep Breathing Institute has helped develop a hardier strain, and these fall spawners will live in freshwater four to five years then go feed off Greenland for awhile.

✔ *TUNA:* Large-scale tuna migrations along the eastern coastline are blamed for the first documented indication of fish egos. What with summer homes off the fashionable Martha's Vineyard and winter homes near Miami, headstrong blue fin tuna may break the traditional tuna pattern of following baitfish and preferred temperature.

✔ *STRIPED BASS:* Mature bass migrate to summer in northern Atlantic waters and return in fall through lure and bait minefields along the Jersey and New York shoreline; the survivors winter in less fashionable areas of the south.

NATURAL ENEMIES OF FISH

✔ *BEARS:* Subscribers to the Disney Channel have seen films of Smokey swatting salmon out of Alaskan waters while cuddly cubs hug each other on the banks. While Buck likes his bears chained to a tree as another roadside attraction, state judges often stop bear hunting so bruins could concentrate on eating more fish and children of bear experts. The U.S. Fish and Game Department has finally proved that bears don't practice catch and release, and the season has been slightly reopened.

✔ *BEAVERS:* For cutting down shade trees that provide safe, cool harbor, these buck-toothed, flat-tailed water devils deserve to be hats for citified fishermen.

✔ *CATS:* The cat chow industry creates billions of pounds of fish gruel each year, and relies on the "snuffing" of innocent fry raised in undersized pens and forced to swim in their own fetid waters.

✔ *CORMORANTS:* A federally protected, big, ugly bird that follows commercial fleets to eat the bycatch or the small fish stirred up by boat motors. Cormorants will even stab an exhausted catch and release fish. One bird can eat two pounds of fillets a day out of a fish farm. These webbed fish killers prefer shad but will take game fish as a second course. In Japan, night fishing with cormorants that swallow the fish just up to a well-secured neck ring almost evens the score.

✔ *COWS:* Indiscriminately destroy riverbanks and spawning beds in their mindless lifestyle. "Beef, it's what's for dinner."

✔ *DOGS:* Eagerly roll on top of dead fish, squeezing out the last dignity.

✔ *DUCKS:* Loon studies have shown that an adult bird can eat up to five trout a day. The national organization, Ducks Unlimited, is quietly funding the growth of Trout Unlimited to prevent a trout rights explosion.

✔ *EAGLES:* All earth-hugging nature TV shows backed with sounds of Peruvian flutes feature eagles sweeping out of a crystalline sky and snatching an unsuspecting salmon out of crystal blue waters and then fade to a commercial for The Nature Conservancy while the national bird rips any fish flesh within easy reach. Earth huggers say that anglers disturb the feedings of the largest winter concentration of bald eagles in the lower U.S and their goal is to turn the designated stretch of river into a bald eagle sanctuary that would ban outboard motors, restrict angler activity, and leave every other fish streamside for eagle midday snacks.

✔ *PELICANS:* The pouches that expand as they eat put these birds on the most wanted list.

✔ *SEA LIONS:* Sea lions eat as much as eight percent of their body weight per day and prefer fresh salmon and steelhead. Commercial fishermen are not sure if in today's legal environment seals and sea lions can be shot in transit and thus use only steel shot, just to be safe.

HATCHERY FISH

To make up for declining habitat, land developers are funding marine biologists to breed replacements species or hatch native spawn in a protected environment to release for commercial or sport fishing. The replacement species include cultivated identical hatchery spawn or special hybrids (discussed elsewhere), while native spawn are collected by biologists who then net and bash adult female fish for their eggs. If the females are not hit too hard, the brain-damaged survivors are sold and shipped to famous fly-fishing schools in the Northeast. The more modern fish sex labs remove eggs by pumping compressed air in and the eggs out of the females. Once the eggs are removed, the air is suctioned out unless the fish have been running too deep for gillnetters. Sperm is extracted from the males in a like fashion, and fish sexologists note that the hatchery fish don't mind the forced premature ejaculation.

Hatchery fish have the necessary hormones to have the biological urge to spawn but have to be taught both to swim upstream and to die. Swimming upstream is taught by placing the young fish in a year-round lap pool, where the fish swim steadily in place against a broad adjustable flow. Hatchery managers in New York State try to create a realistic environment by tossing raw garbage, beer cans, and monofilament into the artificial flow tanks. Officials avoid using catch and release instructor fish as they have no wild habits remaining. A related problem is that schooled hatchery fish grow to appreciate the crowded conditions, and once released, school tightly together in the wild, much to the delight of gill-netters. Teaching the fish to make the long journey and then die has been a joint effort of several universities, who are experimenting with mixing the genes of hearty breed stock with salmon from Scandinavian waters where midwinter suicides are considered an ordinary life passage.

 BUCK'S BONUS TIP: The best time to catch farm fish is after dark.

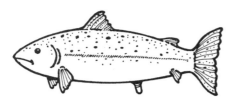

NATIVE FISH
Dorsal fin is fully extended. Other fins straight and healthy, the adipose fin intact. Private parts on bottom of fish erect and proud to be native.

HATCHERY FISH—FIRST GENERATION
Dorsal fin bent or beat up and the adipose fin clipped. Private parts shriveled and rarely erect.

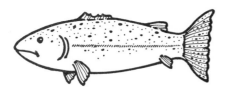

HATCHERY FISH—SECOND GENERATION
Dorsal fin is missing or ragged, yet has a complete adipose fin. Private parts missing or maybe just shy. Easily caught.

In Norway, native Atlantic salmon are outnumbered by salmon of a cultured nature, and threaten to make characteristics of native stock extinct. Native salmon eat krill, which colors the meat pink, so farmers add pigment to the fish chow of hatchery salmon. Marketers promise fish of many colors for wedding banquets, even coordinating with the bride's dress.

In a commercial hatchery, fish can be grown to 1.5 pounds in 18 months, (compared to the typical 30 months required in the wild), by manipulating light and temperature to simulate quickly passing seasons. To maintain the deception, hatchery managers put out their Christmas trees in September, sing carols, and take holiday vacations early.

Compared to other farming operations, hatchery fish are a more efficient foodstuff to raise. For example, 1.8 pounds of fish feed will create 1 pound of fish flesh, while it takes 8 pounds of free U.S. Bureau of Land Management grass to add 1 pound of meat on a steer. The only more efficient animal is your neighbor's dog that creates huge piles for your yard.

HYBRIDS

Fish hybrids are those that are a natural byproduct of fish society and those created late in the lab by gene splicers.

Natural hybrids are accidents of nature while artificial hybrids are specifically designed to improve sport fishing. For example, university researchers are trying to combine the chum salmon's adaptability to salt water with the hardy nature of a Chinook male and have produced a chumook, the sixth species of Pacific salmon. The hybrid is sterilized in the process and does not feel the urge to expend all its energy in a return to the river. This creates a larger fish for the saltwater fisherman.

In Michigan, U.S. Department of Natural Resources and university researchers have stocked sterile Chinook salmon in the Great Lakes. Much like the Norwegian bachelor farmers who fish the lakes, these triploids don't develop complete reproductive organs yet will fatten up quickly and hang around the grange for all the potluck dinners.

Freshwater crosses include northern pike and muskies (tiger muskies), white and striped bass (wipers), saugers and walleyes (saugeyes), and male brown trout and female lake trout (splakes). Fishery biologists trying to create pan fish that live longer and grow bigger but don't mature sexually are being closely watched by a Vatican study group and all fathers with teenage daughters.

In addition to crossbreeding to produce a better mix of social behaviors and just larger fish overall, other scientists are looking to combine the best of physical characteristics:

BIGGER FISH LIPS: In an effort to avoid placing second, tournament biologists have admitted to injecting collagen in planted bass for an easier catch and a more youthful appearance. Once injected, the biologist molds the material to force a smile, a frown, or even a harelip depending on the sense of humor of those involved.

SPECIAL PURPOSE HYBRIDS: Frustrated by unfair lawsuits and bad press, pit bull owners have turned their attention to aquarium fish and have underwritten gene splicing to produce a pit bullhead. Mixing the more aggressive dogfish genes with the common bullhead, hybrid owners are placing their aquariums on open windowsills. Citing a case in New York where a pit bullhead ripped off the ear and part of the scalp of a three-year-old

Siamese cat, the National Hair Ball Lovers Association is requesting legislation to stop this "criminal" crossbreeding.

BYCATCH FISH

Bycatch are the fish you did not set out to catch. Remember when you used to go out for walleyes or any other game fish and those old perch would grab your bait and swallow it deep? You would shake the line hoping the hook would pull out or you'd flip the old cane pole in reverse and splat the fish on the ground behind you. Next you'd step on the head, rip the hook out sideways, hoping to see a live shiner minnow or wiggly worm. Since bycatch fish are not normally listed in the regulations, it's not clear if there are any rules concerning these extra fish. Without clarification, just go about minding your own business.

THE LEVIATHANS

The historical role of really big fish has been to hang fish flesh on the bones of scripture. Fish are ancient things, swimming around in the primordial sea long before your mother-in-law walked upright. The earliest fish one of Buck's ancestors caught was a coelacanth, four hundred million years old, which made it difficult to eat without boiling. Lungfish are their closest living relatives, and both species survive today as the closest living relatives to the early amphibians. Scientists are wondering why these two fish haven't changed over the centuries but then again, fishermen's wives ask the same question about their husbands.

STURGEONS: There are seven U.S. species and two genera, Atlantic to Pacific of this monster. A sturgeon's mouth has feelers that look like a mother superior's mustache. They are an anadromous spawner, beginning in the spring with females dropping up to two million eggs in swift water. At this time, descendants of the Beluga family go diving and scrape the eggs into small cans for shipping to food snots around the world.

CANADIAN LEVIATHAN STORIES: In Kelowna, B.C., reports of a seventy-foot sea serpent, or "Ogopogo," living in Okanogan Lake circulate in the same press kit with news of a balanced federal budget and a good-tasting Canadian wine. Japanese film crews have recorded a large object on sonar amid reports that the Canadian Royal Navy Submarine Service has misplaced one of their coal-burning vessels. Canadian fisheries experts continue to interview boaters who've sighted the freshwater trophy but disqualify all with blood alcohol levels over 10.0, which leaves an abandoned three-year-old husky named King as the only reliable witness to date.

FISH THAT WANT TO HURT YOU

A kid growing up in the Midwest and sitting behind a cane pole would pray to the fish gods that whatever was pulling the bobber down wasn't a bullhead. You know, those black, big-headed fishlike blood buckets with whiskers full of poison. If nobody was around, you'd cut the line as soon as you saw their slime helmets break the surface once gut-hooked or sell it to someone from Iowa. The white meat of the bullhead is fine eating but you must skin them by driving a nail through the head, cutting a ring around it, and pulling the skin off. What remains is a big, ugly black head with ominous tentacles, which if touched, makes your nuts fall off.

Once you've almost gotten used to bullheads, you learn that there are over one thousand species of fresh- and saltwater catfish. The more exotic of these can climb walls with their lips (much to the surprise of South American cliff dwellers), while others will lay under a riverbank with dorsals and pectorals erect, full of venom. Catfish venom won't kill a healthy Buckster but can produce the nausea and cramps associated with a mother-in-law visit.

There are other aquatic troublemakers: sea anemones, stingrays with tails that drive their point home, and needlefish that come out of the water and impale you to your cabin wall. Even a sponge can give you a rash and that's why God made women to do the dishes.

NEITHER FISH NOR FOWL

Responding to the no fuss–no muss, American need to avoid any unpleasantness in life, the Japanese created a seafood product called surimi. Vacuumed from ocean bottoms, this fishy product is cleaned, dehydrated, deflavored, and reshaped into fishlike products with artificial colorings and flavorings.

Sushi is a combination of vinegary rice, lightly seasoned vegetables, and real or imagined seafood, all wrapped in seaweed.

Sashimi is raw tuna, traditionally served with wasabi extracted from the Great Wasabi open pit mines in northern Minnesota.

LOOKING
FOR
FISH

WHAT'S IN A NAME?

Without scientific proof that fish care or have any sense of place, fishermen build importance and mystique around any successful fishing hole. Up to this time, they've had to rely on the names given to the waters by the State Department of Lake Names. In many states you'll find lakes with names like Round, Mud, Long, Birch, Clear, and Lilly. The rivers can be locational like Sawmill Creek, or candid like Dead Fish Creek. The Golden Ponds have gone Hollywood.

In the Northeast, conservation groups are renaming lesser-known waters after prominent Catskill fly fishermen. Those selected are buried along the edge of the rivers bearing their names or allowed one last swim upstream to the headwaters to expire on the gravel beds. Several clubs offer cremation services and, with no argument from the immediate family, the deceased are flash-cooked while in their waders so the ashes can be molded into something finally useful, like a condom.

CLASSIFICATION

In an effort to classify and collect experiences according to some kind of logbook, both government and support groups are labeling all bodies of water. Under the U.S. Wild and Scenic River designation, streams are to be kept essentially as they are with no dams permitted, unless the dam builders have two long teeth, a broad, flat tail, and a pass from the beaver hat lobby.

FEDERAL DESIGNATIONS

✔ *WILD STREAMS:* No road building can occur within one-quarter mile of either side of the river. To get to the river, a fisherman must walk in the footsteps of his predecessors, and if there are no predecessors, the steps must be either back-raked (if grass) or dusted. You cannot take a leak in a wild river. Either hold it or call PETA's Natural Adult Diaper Service.

✔ *SCENIC STREAMS:* Views are to be protected and logging may occur in the general area but not in the river itself. No clear-cutting is allowed, period. Well, maybe a little, but only if there are no spotted owl nests in the trees. On catch and release only streams, the view is to be retained both from the banks outward and inwards toward the soul of the stream.

✔ *RECREATIONAL STREAMS:* Fishing, hunting, and boating can continue to occur under this protection. Logging and agriculture can coexist as long as they don't cause erosion or degrade the river and its banks. If you are shooting carp from your dinghy, it's not clear if you are allowed to blast a fillet off that longhorn edging into your fishing hole. If precedent reigns, don't pull the trigger in Montana or Texas.

SAMPLE STATE DESIGNATIONS

✔ *WASHINGTON:* Starting to classify "quality" trout fishing waters. Anglers flailing at these almost fifty streams and lakes can expect to find larger, happier trout but no bait-fishing, a few fly fishing only, and low creel limits if not catch and release.

✔ *NORTH CAROLINA:* Has Outstanding Resource Waters (ORW) and High-Quality Waters (HQW). ORW have high recreational and/or ecological values, such as great overall fishing, or they're where some troubled soul jumped off the Tallahatchie Bridge. HQW have restricted use. For example, if the water is to be used for a municipal water supply, only residents of that community can swim or take a leak in those waters.

✔ *YELLOWSTONE:* Friends of the First Park have announced plans to reintroduce wild cutthroat into the famous rivers of Yellowstone. Local motel owners and fly tiers are protesting the idea, stating that the introduction would have wild fish eating the catch and release fry and forcing the pre-fished adults to the shallows where distaff fly fishermen could club them at night while awash in properly stirred, not shaken, martinis.

ARTIFICIAL HABITAT

In the United States, there is a long history of creating artificial reefs for healthy spawning habitat along the East Coast, and now many coastal states have artificial reef programs. Example: Alaska's Oil Tanker Reef System.

An inexpensive, modern way to create a pan fish environment is to collect, clean, drill holes in, and anchor used rubber tires. While the installation is wet and heavy work, the tire beds are proven pan fish attractors and hide the unrecyclable shame of the auto industry.

A more popular method is to use natural items such as discarded Christmas trees encased in five-gallon buckets filled with cement. While they may be bulky and prickly to install, the five- to six-foot trees are natural cover, especially when grouped together in a circle. It's not clear if the lights are to be left on. Certainly a little tinsel won't hurt.

In the lakes near gambling casinos and large Italian populations, the planting of local hoodlums has provided local fish species with cover and food at the same time. Individuals who fall out of favor have their handmade alligator shoes encased in five-gallon buckets of cement. Labor union officials based in Fort Lauderdale, Florida, have constructed their own underwater tournament area, dubbing it the Jimmy Hoffa Marine Park after the familiar face of one of the individuals drifting guard at the watery gate.

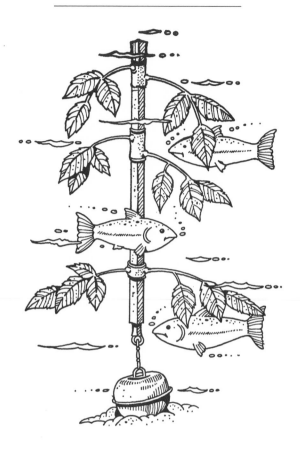

Artificial fish attractors are available that are weighted and tested to attract most of the smaller species. In small quantities, however, fish attractors only concentrate the existing fish rather than build the population. Different conservation groups are building forests of PVC pipe and plastic leaves, rolling plastic snow fence into cylinders and weighting the bottoms for anchoring in groups, or just bundling larger plastic pipe for catfish and other bottom dwellers. In certain areas along the East Coast, there is a severe shorting of housing habitat, especially in the early rent-control attractors, and reports of illegal key fees are surfacing.

WHAT FRESHWATER FISH ARE LIKE

Over 99 percent of all freshwater on this earth is stored in the glaciers up north, and the fish found in those frozen waters will keep until you get there. The remaining 1 percent of freshwater is found either on the earth's surface or under the earth's surface as groundwater. To fish groundwater successfully, you'll have to drop your line down a well.

Generally speaking, freshwater fish are less concerned about speed since they don't migrate far and freshwater predators are fewer and smaller. Often the difference between a baitfish and a fly fisherman's game fish is small indeed.

Buck has assembled the most useful information about the most popular freshwater game fish and put it in alphabetical order for easy referencing. If there are not entries for a certain letter, Buck moves on to a letter that will accommodate entries. (Editor's note: Buck has more than enough paper to make his case.) Buck does know the entire alphabet and recites it as part of his opening remarks for his summer Wilderness School.

In the beginning there was no A, unless you count the A-hole flailing away upstream . . .

✔ *BASS:*
- *LARGEMOUTH:* Probably the most popular game fish in the U.S. and a member of the sunfish family. In tournaments, bucket mouths are filled with lead sinkers that can weigh more than twenty pounds (twenty deciliters in Canada). Hawgs eat small birds, ducklings, and old people's digits, and hold tight and deep in the fall when adult ducks with short memories stop over on their way south. Along with their little brother described below, black bass have the misfortune to have angler societies dedicated to their demise.
- *SMALLMOUTH:* A bronzed warrior of diminished size marked with vertical stripes. Called achigan by the Algonquins to acknowledge its ferocity. In Quebec, bass fishermen are called *achigan a petit bouche* or *cul de cheval.*

- *SILVER OR WHITE BASS:* Bred with striped bass stocked in southern reservoirs to empty the barber shops and park benches.
- *SPOTTED:* The three subspecies are the northern, the Alabama, and the white. Of the three, the Alabama bass is easiest to recognize with its closely set eyes, extended lower jawbone, and genuine appreciation for front-porch banjo music.

✔ *BUFFALO:* A member of the salmon family to an angler from Ohio—both members of the sucker family.

✔ *BURBOT:* A fancy name for ling, the freshwater codfish. It lives cold and deep, feeds at night, and spawns midwinter, much like those who specialize in this fish. With its long, slender chin barbel, the burbot looks like a Vietnamese elder. Without an AK-47, that is.

✔ *BULLHEAD:* Distinguished little brother of the catfish family, and comes in black, brown, and yellow. One of Buck's childhood neighbors was nicknamed "Bullhead" for his ability to get his head stuck inside a potato chip can.

✔ *CARP:* Wrongly titled a rough or trash fish, these gentle giants were first domesticated in Europe and Asia where they were ridden by small aquatic warlords. Carp were introduced into the United States in the late 1800s as part of a government subsidy program. Once the politicians saw how popular they were and how fast they multiplied, carp were introduced into their home district fishing holes via congressional "fish barrel" projects. Predictably, carp overpopulated many waters. When not used as fertilizer for your rose bushes, carp is used to make gefilte fish, a Jewish fish ball thrown at all the traditional holiday food fights.

✔ *CATFISH:* Comes from the Ictaluridae family, a Latin word meaning "American heiress's vagina," I think. With twenty four different kinds in the

United States alone, the most active is the channel cat, and the largest are the blue catfish and the flathead. (See Fish That Will Hurt You.) Fishermen who grapple the largest catfish are easily recognized by their artificial limbs.

 BUCK'S BONUS TIP: Catfish whiskers are heaviest at the end of the day. Buck recommends the new five-blade razor.

✔ *CRAPPIES:* White and black crappies are small, flat fish that look like fish a kid would draw. They school nicely and are best caught with an older brother named Dave out of a seventeen-foot Herter's square stern canoe, with minnows and hooks with bobbers. For those who can count on both hands, the black has seven spines on its dorsal fin, while the white has six and a shorter dorsal fin. For those counting, on the white crappie, the distance from the front of the dorsal fin to the eye is longer than the length of the fin itself. On the black, it's the same, more or less. Unless you use the metric system.

✔ *DOGFISH:* Contrary to popular belief, dogfish do not change into snakes under a full moon. It has to be a new moon.

✔ *EEL:* Europeans and Asians prize eels, and since we have opened wide the doors at Ellis Island, this fish is rising in popularity. There are reports that young Italian "made" men strap eels to an upper thigh before pulling guard duty outside the social clubs.

✔ *FLUSHER:* The huge feces-eating goldfish found in New York City's sewer system. Reserve for family reunion cookouts.

✔ *GAR:* A charter member of the original trash fish family that early Western settlers killed as varmints. There are six models: The Florida gar, the spotted gar, the alligator gar (last seen up to ten feet long, over three hundred pounds, and with a child's leg hanging out its snout), Teri Garr, and the long-nose and short-nose gars.

✔ *MUSKELLUNGE:* Lunkers up to sixty pounds are caught mid-afternoon when most bass fishermen are into the second rack of beer. Muskies have been successfully crossbred with the smaller northern pike females. Hatchery managers defend the inbreeding by noting how common retardation is among the royal political families of the Northeast and how they keep getting reelected.

✔ *PADDLEFISH:* Found only in the Missouri-Mississippi river basin, these are the most primitive of the bony fish and native only to North America. The distinguishing feature is the long, flat snout, extending up to one-third of its entire length. Although it's called a bony fish, it's almost all cartilage, much like your nose. In fact, since it's already one third nose and almost three-thirds nose material, it could be called a nose fish. Buck will put through the necessary paperwork. You'd think they'd spend their entire life sneezing, what with the boogers found in those rivers.

✔ PERCH: The perch family is known for a completely divided back fin and has three principal groupings: the darter family, the walleye/sauger bunch, and the yellow perch family.
   • *DARTER:* A protected small fish with the power and history to slow or stop major dams and reclamation projects. Tasty as smelt when deep-fried.
   • *WALLEYES:* The wild bunch at a perch family reunion and are described under W.
   • *YELLOW PERCH:* There are two main groups, yellow and white. Perch have rich meat but their skin seems hairy, especially if you leave them in the bottom of the aluminum boat all sunny day long. During the day,

they'll feed in schools under your boat and at night will try to figure out where you and your worms will be tomorrow.

✔ *PIKE:* The three more popular pike are the northern pike, the muskellunge (see again under M, just before N), and the chain pickerel. The northern pike (or snake or jacks) are long, lean, mean eating machines. Northerns hatch early to eat muskie fry, which makes parent muskies even meaner. The current world record northern is over 60 pounds. Isaac Walton spoke of great pike over 550 pounds in his famous treatise but hid behind his pig latin as to the exact whereabouts.

✔ *SALMON:* Buck knows this species is also in the saltwater section, but in the 1960s, coho salmon were introduced into Lake Michigan as baitfish for the popular game fish, the sea lamprey. The salmon instead ate all the alewives, which made up most of the lake biomass. Once the cohos made it, Chinook were added, and now both Lakes Huron and Michigan have good salmon fisheries with more than the yearly adult requirement of mercury. At high levels, mercury can trigger memory and hearing loss, slurred speech, lack of coordination, and reproductive problems which make it hard to diagnose from an ordinary bass fisherman.

✔ *SMELT:* While closely related to the salmon, smelt are a small, slender minnow, many of which want to migrate into freshwater in the spring to spawn but are surprised by fishermen working the banks and mouths of rivers with spotlights, dip nets, and cheap whiskey. Smelt is served on Friday nights in Elk's clubs across the country—all you can eat, beverages extra. Do you want fries with that?

✔ *STRIPERS (OR STRIPED BASS):* Marked with alternating rows of black and white scales and are active year-round so unemployed people in the South can at least fish. Originally an ocean fish but accidentally trapped behind a dam in South Carolina and now a success story. In spring, male stripers head up river with the old lady to lend support during the spawn then retreat down-stream to the lake to sleep off the summer.

✔ *STURGEON:* The largest freshwater fish on the earth. In the 1800s, lake sturgeons were prized by the natives but taken by others for oil in paints, smoked to feed cheap laborers, and killed to make a material called isinglass from the backbone to clarify European wines. The slaughter stopped once a German sommelier told a French vintner to just lay the bottles on their sides. Prized for their eggs for both the table and the hatchery, sturgeons prefer to die than give up their spawn voluntarily.

✔ *SUCKERS:* The bad news is that there are over seventy species of suckers in North America. The good news is that you are unlikely to catch all of them in one day. Clearly a fish without intelligent design. For example, the fish gods put the teeth in the throat instead of the jawbone. Who knows what other mistakes those practical jokers made? White suckers are the most prevalent and are commonly used to rub fresh oil into dog coats.

✔ *SUNFISH (OR BREAM IN THE SOUTH):* Small, round, flat fish often weighing less than half a pound, but real scrappers in light gear when guarding the nursery. Principal models are redbreast, green, red ear, pumpkinseed, and bluegill. An altogether too short description of one of the most popular training fish.

✔ *TILAPIA:* The fish of the future, commercially raised and already a million served. Originally from the Middle East, tilapia is said to be the fish Jesus fed to his disciples at the Sea of Galilee, and that same fish, albeit fresher, was thought to be found in Buck's last fishwich at the local drive-through. The national fish of Israel and an important part of the Palestinian food stamp program.

BUCK'S BONUS TIP: According to the latest papal pronouncement, fishing is no longer a sin if accompanied by a 5 percent increase in tithing or your wife going off the pill.

✔ *TROUT:* Divided into the char group (Arctic chars, brook, Dolly Varden, lake, and Sunapee) and the no char, true trout group. The char group Salvelinus spawn in the fall while the western group of the Salmonidae family spawns in early spring and summer. Arctic char and Dolly Varden look so much alike that most mothers can't tell the difference. Dolly Vardens are typically noted for their large breasts and live in country western waters.

- *BROOK TROUT:* A speckled native trout that welcomed Chris Columbus and the pilgrims to our shores. Actually a char, usually small and beautiful in full fall foliage. No black spots and wild in the Southeast. Won't tell where.

- *BROWN TROUT:* European transplants and stocked in American rivers to bring high culture to our waters. Adverse public sentiment during the Big War caused the German browns to petition to be named brown trout. Like their human counterparts, they can withstand heat better than other trout, and in large bodies of water they can grow up past forty pounds. Brown trout will spawn either in the fall or winter. Won't tell you when. There has to be a few mysteries.

- *CUTTHROAT TROUT:* So named by red-orange slashes on the bottom of the lower jaw. Not prized by fly fishermen (using Mepps spinners) since they won't jump unless your camcorder has an automatic focus.

- *GOLDEN TROUT:* First described by the dope-smoking cults and confirmed by Presbyterians that only drink decaf, these small beauties were once transplanted to other high alpine lakes. Since the golden trout has been selected as California's state fish, like much of its rebel culture, the trout cannot be transplanted in other states.

- *MACKINAW OR LAKE TROUT:* The big boys with forked tails that patrol cool northern waters only. Called togue in Maine and only the

Algonquins know why and they won't tell until L.L. Bean declares the moccasin the Original Maine Hunting Boot.

- *RAINBOW TROUT:* Identified by their rose-colored band and stocked in many Midwestern and eastern waters. Originally called *Salmo gairdneri* like steelhead, DNA studies show rainbows to be closely related to the Pacific genus *Oncorhynchus*. If so, the species name would revert back to the original *mykiss* and will be listed as salmon under the rainbow.

- *SUNAPEE TROUT:* Descendant of the eastern brook trout that first lived in Sunapee Lake, Sunapee, New Hampshire, which was not important then and certainly isn't now, except to the direct descendants of Mr. Sunapee, who have a few lakefront lots to sell.

✔ *STEELHEADS:* Another freshwater contender. Sound like foundry workers but are actually migrating rainbows. They view their little rainbow cousins in much the same way that big farm boys look at their city cousins. Steelheads have been planted in the Great Lakes and programmed to spawn-start the tourist season.

✔ *WALLEYE:* The largest member of the perch world and not a walleyed pike. So expensive at the supermarket, you might as well catch them yourself. This night owl has extra sensitive eyes and thus prefers cool, dimly lit waters. Number one species in the Midwest, except Wisconsin where bottle bass has reigned supreme since Jet Skies were discovered.

✔ *WHITEFISH:* Most commonly found smoked in supermarkets. Ciscoes are small whitefish, all with the dazed look of a catch and release trout.

WHAT SALTWATER FISH ARE LIKE

Saltwater fish are bigger and stronger than freshwater fish. Saltwater fishermen are bigger and stronger and quite often better looking than freshwater fishermen.

✔ *ALBACORE:* These long-range travelers move through all oceans in a band between forty degrees south and north latitude. The white meat has the highest commercial value of any tuna. Albacore don't have bladders to provide buoyancy and must move forward for lift by sticking out their extra long pectoral fins, which makes for a mighty long day.

✔ *BARRACUDA:* Associated with ciguatera poisoning in the Atlantic but clean as a whistle in the Pacific. Retailers recommend cooking with the skin on as the wrappers are difficult to remove. In the food world, barracuda rate just ahead of skunk. Also another name for an upwardly mobile career woman.

✔ *BILLFISH:* A hot-issue fish family. Commercial catch, possession, and sales of billfish are banned except for swordfish. Blue and white marlin and all sailfish are declared recreational species, and the commercial take has a tolerance of 15 percent undersize fish per landing or maybe fifty-four undersize fish per boat per day. Or was it fifteen undersize fishermen fifty-four minutes late in landing?

    • *ATLANTIC SAILFISH:* Likes warm water and weighs fifty to sixty pounds. A most abundant sailfish found near shore. Pacific sailfish are larger, give better photo, and make a much nicer trophy for the office or, if married, the garage.

    • *MARLIN:* White marlin average fifty pounds and have rounded pectoral fin tips. While smaller than a blue marlin, the white is a better fighter especially as a 150-pounder, so you can imagine what a fighter it would be if it weighed 10,000 pounds, which it can't. Pay attention. Blue marlin can go as high as 2,000 pounds, are found on both coats and identified by pointed dorsal, pectoral, and anal fins. Fortunately, Japanese soup-makers want no part of a 2,000-pound anal fin. Any black marlin over 300 pounds is a female and to be accorded respect. The striped marlin is a very common billfish along warm Pacific waters and the Marlin 39A rifle is a great .22 rifle to shoot that damn squirrel emptying your bird feeder.

- *SWORDFISH:* Named *Xiphiasgladius* for short Roman sword, found along both coasts, weighing up to a ton, and identified by its smooth, flat sword and high menu prices. These pelagic loners will attack a boat if the bait isn't presented properly.

✔ *BLUEFISH:* The young small "snappers" grow into twenty-five-pound choppers. Bluefish is thought to be the most important saltwater recreational fish. When eating as a school in surf, they have been known to bite bathers. Will leave an oily slick on the water, depending on whom or what they are eating, with major oil slicks reported off Italy. Blues are good fighters, like to jump, and are best smoked. Let me take that back, best left with the locals and then you go get smoked.

✔ *COD:* Important historical fish. Codpieces were first worn by Africans and then feminist frontier women. The number one fish consumed, frozen or unfrozen (not canned), in the United States and usually found breaded (in the grocery freezers, not in the water, dummy!). Scrod is a size of cod, not a rash in the groin area.

✔ *DOLPHIN:* These may get as big as one hundred pounds, a common size along the Atlantic Coast and Gulf of Mexico, but in Hawaii only reach two to five pounds. They look like they ran into a brick wall. Called mahi mahi in Hawaii, dorado in Latin America, and fish sticks in Wisconsin.

✔ *DRUM:* A croaker that produces a sound by vibrating a muscle near its swim bladder. Red drum is North Carolina's state fish, and large red drums are called bull reds even if they are females. These "redfish" are strong tasting, infested with worms, and blackened to serve to tourists who think chicory is a kind of coffee bean. The good news is that the worms are higher in protein than the fish. The least important member is the weakfish, commonly called squeteaque by the locals, and they sure know what they are talking about.

✔ *GROUPER:* This member of the Serranidae family starts life as a female and changes to a male after a few years of seeing how difficult it is to get promoted in a male-dominated advertising industry. Large groupers weighing as much as seven hundred pounds are called jewfish, which just goes to show you.

✔ *HALIBUT:* The largest flat-bottom feeder provides all the action of a garage door yet sets the standard on how good fish can taste. The cheeks are considered a delicacy, and Japanese trawlers are devising ways to suck out the cheeks without keeping the rest. Fish biologists are concerned that de-cheeked fish may not survive and certainly will never smile again.

✔ *JACKS:* These warm-water fish with deep forked caudal fins are found along the Atlantic coast and in the Gulf of Mexico. The larger ones schooled near Geraldo as he publicly plundered the Andrea Doria. Pacific amberjack usually has worms but even the lower orders must have a life.

✔ *KILLER SHARKS:* See *Jaws,* especially the first one with Robert Shaw.

✔ *LINGCOD:* The common bottom fish of the Pacific Northwest, ranging as far south as Baja California and north to Alaska. These fish are what salmon charter party boats will put you onto if they can't find real fish. If your charter captain promises a fish or a rain check, he'll make sure you get one of these to get him off the hook.

✔ *MACKEREL:* Sighting this fish is fraught with religious significance and there is just one exclamation appropriate at such moments. A member of the family that includes tuna and bonito. The wahoo is the most desirable eating. The rest, including the Atlantic mackerels, are best as cut bait for real fish. Called a workingman's fish, but don't let those thugs hear you say that.

✔ *MAHI MAHI:* The Hawaiian name for dolphin. It is not the mammal dolphin or porpoise. There have been rumors that an occasional actor from Dolphin Land ends up as fish-and-chips if they don't perform properly in front of sellout crowds.

✔ *MARLIN:* See billfish. The fastest, largest oceangoing bony fish. Their bodies are very complex as key parts are kept at temperatures above those of the water they swim in. For example, their eyes and brains are warmed by a heater organ associated with one of the eye muscles. This defroster is important, particularly during a cold, snowy northeaster. Also a fine firearm manufacturer. *See Buck's Complete Guide to Deer Hunting.*

✔ *POLLACK:* A friend of the Cod family and found in any Wisconsin tavern, eating hard-boiled eggs and beef jerky with broken yellow teeth.

✔ *SALMON:* The Northwest Indian name for fish, loosely translated as "odor in teepee coming from in-laws visiting more than three moons." Of the six species of Pacific salmon (*Oncorhynchus*), five are found on the West Coast and a sixth (*O. Driftnetstolefishka*) found in the holds of dark-running Japanese boats.
  • *ATLANTIC SALMON, SALOMO SOLAR:* Originally used as fertilizer, this accounts for the difference in taste from Pacific salmon. In just one win-

ter at sea, will grow to four pounds and become a grilse, a purposeful misspelling of the Weber outdoor appliance many end up on. Most will, however, spend two or three winters at sea, adding six to eight pounds, or add another winter to push the scale up to as much as thirty pounds. Late bloomers that hang around up to six winters can weigh up to seventy pounds and a few developmentally disabled never leave the sea and eventually explode, setting off the alarm clock in the Canadian coal-burning submarine asleep somewhere off Newfoundland.

- *BOOT SALMON, O. VERLIMITA:* A very popular three- to five-pound sport salmon species found in hip boots and waders of nonresidents, brothers-in-law, and natives.

- *CHINOOK SALMON, O. TSHAWYTSCHA:* The king of salmon. Ranging as far south as California and north to Nome, Alaska, these large migrators school near shorelines and tempt small boats into deep, distant dangerous waters. Two basic flesh colors are white and red salmon turn pink because they eat shrimp, crab, and krill which contain carotenoid. The white king salmon eat either the other white meat or have their meat lightened by the wood pulp bleaching operation upriver.

- *CHUM OR DOG SALMON, O. KETA:* They range up to thirty to thirty-five pounds, and while a popular commercial fish, famous Alaskan guides like P. Richter take unsuspecting Seattle fishermen to the Yukon River for "King Chum" salmon just to collect exorbitant guide fees and more than his share of Jack Daniel's adult breakfast beverages.

- *COHO SALMON, O. KISUTCH:* Silvers weigh at most thirty pounds but without a doubt are the most interesting sport fishing salmon to catch. A premium boot salmon (see above).

- *HUCHO HUCHO TAIMEN:* The largest salmon in the world, the taimen, is now being sought by sport-fishermen. Some of the fish most recently taken easily exceed 100 pounds and even larger trophies have been described between big gulps of potato vodka. The largest taken commercially was in Siberia, weighing 251 pounds and measuring 7 feet long. The taimen salmon eats other salmon, ducks and huskies, and is rumored to have consumed more than one small Siberian icehouse wife. Taimen salmon do not die after spawning and can live up to 100 years. By practicing catch and release, it's possible for one fisherman to catch the same fish year in and out and for the fish to outlive the fisherman, which is good.

- *PINK SALMON, O. GORBUSCHA:* The smallest salmon, weighing one to ten pounds, or more. In the Pacific Northwest, they run only in odd-numbered years, 2001, 2003, and 2005 unless it's a leap year. In full spawn, the male shows greenish brown colors while the female remains her cranky old self.

- *SOCKEYE SALMON, O. NERKA:* Reds are good eating, average seven pounds, and are largely a commercial fish. Usually packaged in a wooden box with Indian longhouse logos for shipping to relatives in the Midwest who prefer their salmon in a can.

✔ *SHARKS:* White sharks can get as big as two tons and these man-eaters are found where you least expect them. Smaller sharks like the very common sandbar eat only small surfers.

✔ *SNAPPER:* This family has over 185 members. Red snapper is not a red-headed "hottie," it's best blackened with that big Cajun's spices. Gulf shrimp fishermen have developed a strong taste for red snapper and favor a dish called "bouillabaisse of bycatch."

✔ *SNOOK:* Called *brochet de mer* by the French and, *bon ami*, don't be snookered by their cultural nonsense.

✔ *STRIPED BASS (ATLANTIC):* A commercially depleted stock with a high tolerance for toxins and enjoy passing on the altered genetic code with abandon. Hybrid striped bass are bred in aquaculture and then abandoned at the fish market.

✔ *TARPON:* Large scale(d) sport fish. Frustrated old salts fish with Navy depth charges while tarpon spawn offshore. The females are so fertile their image appears on the entire Vatican motor-pool, including the Pope-Mobile.

✔ *TUNA:* Yellowfin tuna are an international warm-blooded species that unfortunately likes swimming with porpoises in temperate waters. Usually ends up in a casserole. The byproducts usually end up in a cat dish. Bluefin tuna are the giants, reaching a weight of up to a ton. Bluefin have short pectorals and the highest value to the Japanese fish buyer with even shorter pectorals.

✔ *WAHOO:* Named the greyhound of the sea for its ability to make all stops. Named Ono by Hawaiians and they sure said a mouthful there. Usually caught by yahoos.

FISHE**R**MEN
AND
FISHERPERSONS

STATISTICAL PROFILE

The average fisherman fishes less than thirty days a year so it's hard to imagine why a wife would object to so few days. There is little available research on what days of the week the fishing was done, or how long the lawn was on those same days. More than half of the fishermen reported that they made more than the U.S. media income. Buck's good fishing buddies said that their person financial information was none of your business and went one step further by saying that the IRS could go tax themselves.

BECAUSE THE POPE SAID SO

Where great religions jostle for market share, fish play an important role in marketing plans. In the 1800s, Catholics were having trouble holding onto their faithful, who were moving west to cattle ranch and turn Lutheran at the Missouri synod tollbooths. For this and other reasons, the Pope decided to punish those renegades by cutting into their business with a ban on red meat on a major weekend night. He realized too late how that would help Frank Perdue and all his chickens. The only exceptions to the meatless Friday were isolated pagan celebrations such as Saint Paddy's Day (corned beef and cabbage), and the rougher Italian get-togethers, such as the Saint Valentine's Day Massacre.

The bible can be considered the first fishing guidebook. If you have the money to own both the Bible and this guidebook, buy two of Buck's and steal the Gideon Bible from your next hotel room. If you stay in a Marriott Hotel, you are allowed to take the Bible and The Story of the Marriott Family. If you can prove you read the entire Marriott story without checking out early and moving over to the Hilton, they will send you a complete set of hotel towels and washcloths, much like the ones you already have.

The fishing stories in the Bible are called parables, from the great philosopher Parabus, who was a difficult guest at toga parties because of his long-winded, often dull anecdotes. King James admitted in his autobiography (now out of print) that the editing of the parables was the most difficult task in his version of the Good Book.

The important fish parables from the Bible are:

Genesis 9:2-3, "...and all the fish of the sea, into your hands are given."
ANALYSIS: Saint Gillnetter's reading of the Bible claims that only commercial long liners and purse seiners are included here. The recreational fisherman's (or Saint Gaffer's) reading disputes this by continuing the verse with:

"Every moving thing that is alive shall be food for you."
ANALYSIS: This unfortunately includes carp.

Matthew 28:19-20, "...follow me and I will make you fishermen."
ANALYSIS: Disregard this passage as the TV evangelists have already gillnetted far too many of the unsuspecting.

Cars that have accepted Jesus Christ as their personal mechanic sport the shape of a fish, usually mounted just above the Bob's Buick Barn insignia. This symbol is good for free parking at most synagogues. A gold plated symbol indicates a tournament angler, and multiple schooling symbols signify either good grades at church school or a good meat fisherman.

Cradle Catholics have long been told that Friday was the day you had to eat fish. While never written down anywhere, this practice was intended by the Vatican to support the Catholic fishing industry. Papal family planners noted the birth rates of fishing families and decided to encourage their seasonal hatch.

If threatened with communion wine shortages, a good Catholic will confess that there is an unwritten biblical injunction against eating meat of the hoofed animal before the Sabbath. The original plan by Vatican strategists was to enforce the ban for the entire weekend, but a successful lobbying effort by the National Association of Surf and Turf Specials pushed the Holy See to focus on the less important Friday night. The Holy advice was simple but direct: Eat fish on Friday or die Lutheran! Under pressure from the more wealthy parishioners, priests included lobster and crab on the faithful's "fresh sheet." For the less fortunate, tuna fish casseroles were recommended, and in celebration, the Portuguese fishing fleet in San Diego flew victory dolphins from their yardarms. The remaining faithful were assigned to choose from the category loosely termed "white fish," nicknamed cod or Pollack, all euphemisms for a meat that has no flavor even when surrounded by an attractive breaded jacket.

If you were a Protestant living in a Catholic neighborhood, empathy casseroles were served on Friday night but in forms unknown to the mackerel snappers. In Minnesota, a favorite was salmon loaf, served dry and full of small, round chewable bones. Caught in the fresh, salty brine of a number four can, these finned warriors of the Pacific Northwest would be reshaped into a log and covered with thick liquid. If you were trapped in the housing net of the Pope's fishing fleet, your red meat frenzy would never be interrupted, except by a nagging wish that the Catholic divorcée across the street would open her shades a little wider.

COMMERCIAL FISHERMEN

Commercial fishermen are the hale and hearty sailors who fill our plates with fresh fish. A high risk, often high reward industry, commercial fishing is one of the most dangerous occupations in Alaska, if you don't count stiffing a table dancer in one of Anchorage's better strip clubs.

FISHERWOMEN

Sport anglers have traditionally left the little woman behind on the proverbial shoreline for one good reason: Fishing was often the only activity that you didn't have to listen to her nagging about a new car, new coat, more kids, too many kids, larger house, and missing money from the checking account. On the few occasions that you did include her, Buck knows you picked the nastiest weather, the darkest of nights, the roughest water, and the least likely biting conditions. You did all you could to dissuade her from your private adventures. Too bad. She knows how much fun it is. She doesn't want to be part of your male bonding boat and has split off to form her own fishing groups.

There are now women's fishing organizations that sponsor tournaments along with other membership activities. In the women-only tournaments, sexual privacy is guaranteed but the male press is allowed interviews in the dressing room under the tournament catch and release program. The lady anglers are also lobbying for women-only seasons, but male bass clubs are suing for forced entry.

NEW EQUIPMENT FOR THE LITTLE WOMAN: Since women have smaller hands, shorter arms, more fragile muscles, and recently rediscovered breasts, manufacturers have tooled up for the growth in this market with smaller, more sensitive rods and reels and, at the request of the male guides, a snazzy array of colorful fishing bras. Bait fishermen persist in designing tackle to resemble their women—with heavier butts and larger tippets. With the new interest in fly-fishing, fly fisherwomen are proving that small-breasted women have feelings, too.

NEW TECHNIQUES FOR THE LITTLE WOMAN: Several researchers postulate women fish better because their sex hormones attract fish, and recent records are evidence of that. With female fish traditionally being the larger of the two genders, this angling success may just be another overworked example of networking. Female fisherwomen fish by intuition and significant research shows that a woman's body can be considered a two-legged solar/lunar table. Barometric pressure affects all women, with low pressure causing mood swings and a desire to leave the housework behind. High-pressure systems accompanied by sunlight elevate their feelings and makes them more willing to clean your fish. In closely-knit groups, such as a fly-tying bee, fisherwomen can experience a phenomenon when their individual menstrual cycles occur simultaneously and only a surprise visit by the Chippendale dancers will relieve the pressure. In fact, a small number of large fly fisherwomen standing near preadolescent girls can induce puberty.

COMMERCIAL FISHERWOMEN: Traditional view from the flying bridge is that women should be either waving from the widow's nest as the boat leaves the harbor or have a position on the cannery line. The jury is still out. While working on the Great Lakes as a young seaman, however, Buck noticed that the only women on the big boats were overnight guests from the Order of Royal Painted Ladies of the Shoreline, either a Catholic organization or a chief engineer's union allocation.

SPORT SEX ON THE HIGH AND LOW SEAS

Legislation now requires ship captains or other senior officers to promptly report to the Coast Guard any complaints of a sexual offense aboard any U.S. fishing vessel. The act provides fines and hard time for the good times committed within the U.S. maritime jurisdiction.

Several Alaskan fish processors heap scorn on the legislators who have never "worked a boat on heaving, thrusting seas." The Japanese boats deny carrying women on board, and most Coast Guard observers can't tell the difference between "those pesky drift-netters" anyway. The Canadian fleet simply enjoys having a chance to go out on a nice, sunny day and has agreed not to hose any crewmember while in international waters.

PACIFIC NORTHWEST NORTHWEST INDIANS

In 1974, Judge George Boldt of Washington State decided to split the fish harvest in half between native and non-native fishermen and a copy of this re-interpreted treaty follows.

Treaty

Here ye, Hear ye! Whereas and so as, my officer or rather I the Great White Father in the Other Washington do wish to say to the Great Red Brother Chief of the Northwest shoreline that what is yours is ours except that which doesn't fit our current market needs and not provided in our manifest land quest given the current state of the yen, is whereas and so as to your heathen bare ass so verily I say trust us as we show our utmost good faith toward your savage Indians and your lands and properties shall never be taken from you without your dissent. And not having received a call from you with your consent we whereas figured this treaty was right and just but you may be able to fish like you used to but we'll get back to you on season and limits later and then we'll mint a nickel for your graven image as a subway token of our gratitude to replace all the plugged wooden nickels Canadian trappers give you if you foreswear overuse of peyote because the Great Spirit says overindulgence blurs the message and whereas you used to live in a state of nature unincorporated and fish a lot without limit so be it and fourscore and foreskins, thank you Mammy. Amen. Sealed with my hand. The Great White Father c/o The Big White House on the Prairie, Washington, D.C. Return Postage Guaranteed.

WISCONSIN INDIANS

Back before there was a Wisconsin and a legal age to drink too much bad beer, the Chippewa went about their natural ways, taking fish and game according to tradition and need. While the squaws were back in the teepees tying Indy Rigs, the warriors were throwing fishing spears at walleyes in nearby lakes. This spring harvest fueled the energies and imaginations of the proud Plains Indians who dreamed of never having to make reservations.

When the German immigrants arrived in the mid 1800s, the Indians noticed a new overripe cabbage smell wafting through the hitherto pristine air and called the Great White Father in Washington to establish a treaty to keep the burgermeisters on their side of the lake. The treaties granted exclusive native rights to continue spearing fish (and not sausage makers) and, in a major concession, allowed the Germans to continue to brew substandard beer.

INDIAN FISH ALLOCATIONS

In parts of the country that split the harvest, fishery managers have analyzed court decisions and arrived at complicated but equitable allocations between native and nonnative fishermen.

NATIVE FISHERMEN:
Tribal councils traditionally divide their share of the booty according to bloodline and other important criteria.

✔ *FULL-BLOODED TRIBAL MEMBERS:* 25 percent tribal bloodline
✔ *HALF-BLOODED TRIBAL MEMBERS BUT PAYING FULL DUES:* 25 percent
✔ *BLOODED TRIBAL MEMBERS WITH IDENTITY PROBLEMS:* 25 percent

✔ *HONORARY TRIBAL MEMBERS:* 5 percent

✔ *INDIANS WITHOUT RESERVATIONS:* 5 percent

✔ *THE ESTATE OF CHIEF DAN GEORGE:* 4 percent

✔ *THE ESTATES OF ROY ROGERS, TOM MIX, AND GABBY HAYES:* 4 percent

✔ *DRUGSTORE INDIANS:* 2 percent

✔ *SACRIFICES TO FISH GODS:* 2 percent

✔ *WIFE CANDY:* 2 percent

✔ *SLED DOGS:* 1 percent

✔ *BREEDING STOCK:* 1 percent

NONNATIVE FISHERMEN:

A friendly yet temporary truce between the commercial and recreational fishermen has produced a friendly but temporary decision:

✔ *COMMERCIAL FISHERMEN:* 99 percent

✔ *RECREATIONAL FISHERMEN:* 99 percent

✔ *SPILLAGE AND BREEDING STOCK:* 1 percent

NATIVE CANADIAN FISHERMEN:

In the Great White North, relations between the federal government and the tribes are deteriorating because there are no formal treaties between the tribes and Ottawa. Like their U.S. brothers, the Canadian tribal fishermen are petitioning for expanded rights to catch salmon and steelhead for both commercial reasons and for personal, ceremonial, and religious purposes. One problem with the native tribes' request is the historically high consumption of salmon. Native scholars estimate more than fifteen hundred pounds of salmon per person per year. It's not clear exactly what roles all that fish played, but this scholar promises to tell at the next potlatch.

NONNATIVE CANADIAN FISHERMEN

✔ *IN THE NORTHEAST:* Ever since the Magnuson Act gave both Canada and the United States two hundred miles of free play, the battle over traditional fishing areas continues in the Northeast. U.S. commercial boats spotted illegally in Canadian waters are often chased by armed Mounties in war canoes. The alternative to surrendering to Sergeant Preston is to plead guilty to the U.S. Lacey Act, which carries a hefty fine for carrying seafood caught illegally in foreign waters or requires a promise to marry a hefty farm woman from Maine.

✔ *IN THE NORTHWEST:* Up north, Canadians wish to recognize a 1903 border that cuts off the southern tip of the Alaska Peninsula. The United States prefers the line that runs between each nation's offshore islands, and threatens to route the Exxon Valdez through their waters one more time.

BOY SCOUTS

In earlier, more innocent times, scouting gave you the excuse to sneak off with a cane pole and can of worms, all in an early test of sportsmanship. Your first fish was brought home where your mom politely honored the catch by preparing it for the family table and the scout troop dutifully honored you with the Fishing Merit Badge, which used to look like this.

Scouting in the new millennium is an entirely different story. No leaving junk fish in the bottom of the canoe where, on a hot Minnesota day, they'll bake right past the stench and into a crispy critter than can be thrown at your little sister. No more sticking cherry bombs in the suction cup mouth of a carp. The buzzword around the new campfire, where adult metrosexuals lead off with Earth First! songs, is low-impact camping. The new scout must now cook the catch (if they are allowed to keep it) over a stove, not an open fire. In the latest handbook, the Big Headmaster prepares the new scout for a lifetime spent indoors fixing precious meals for his life partner (or mother). While the National Park Service has no regulations against campfires, their talking head calls the scout policy a "responsible effort" and concludes "if we want a fire in a national park, we'll set it and let it burn. In fact, if you think Yellowstone was a good fire, you haven't seen anything yet."

Originally scouting was to protect boys and young men from the adult world of men "tempted by drink, ruined by gambling, and contaminated by loose women." Since most men have no knowledge of any of these three, they are letting Girl Scouts write their unisex manuals. The new Fishing Merit Badge under consideration in the combined Boy/Girl Scout Headquarters looks like this.

BASS FISHERMEN: IS THERE NO LIMIT?

Members of the Homogenized Fly-Fishing Purists within a Hundred Miles of the World Headquarters of Orvis have taken possession of idle fly-tying vises, hoping to splice model DNA genes of bass fishermen in an effort to genetically influence their traditional resistance to catch and release. Up to this point, efforts have been blocked by super connective tissues between the catch and release wimp gene and the gene that allows bass fishermen to drink beer out of long-neck bottles without using their hands. The Beer Institute, an Alabama-based think tank, has warned that "tampering with what Mother Nature intended" could lean to unknown danger and unexpected darkness.

Trout fly fishermen have discovered that bass fishermen really do enjoy fishing more, and in order to have a few bass left to fish, the New York chapter of Planned Parenthood has announced a program to subsidize Saturday and Sunday open houses in the southern bass states and to appoint selected tavern owners near famous bass lakes as sales agents for extra large condoms. The New York City chapter of Untitled Fly Fishermen has organized a PAC to support the agency efforts and encourage donations earmarked for birth control of bass fishermen.

SCHOOLS

Fishermen school together for two very important reasons—for security and for feeding.

✔ *SECURITY* is the primary bonding device in a large grouping of fishermen.
✔ *FEEDING* is their one stated reason for grouping and when combined with drinking contains the social behavior that most often involved the local authorities.

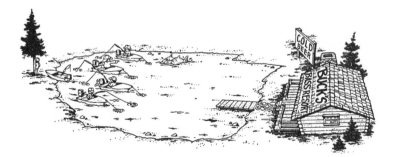

An aerial view of schooling summer fishermen

There are real schools for fishermen, subsidized by tackle manufacturers to get you to commit to major purchases or by famous fishermen who have books, videos, and lures to sell. One of the more popular schools is Buck's fishing school. Two- and three-day fishing schools are being offered for the first time at Buck's Bass Resort. The same curriculum is taught to both classes as Buck has learned that despite what fishing magazines or other schools beg to indicate, the depth of material isn't so great that it can't be taught all at once. Speed-readers may be able to complete the written portions over two cups of coffee. Slower readers may include a donut. Multiple syllable words, directed toward the older angler, are liberally yet slowly sprinkled into the instruction. If the two-day participants refuse or, worse, forget to leave after the shorter instruction, they will be charged for the third day but will receive the special boat decal diploma.

Deluxe lodging is available at Buck's Beautiful Bass Resort on Big Babe Lake in northernmost Minnesota. The log cabin lodge on the shores of the finest fishing lake within 20 miles or so features comfortable guest rooms, the popular Valhalla Lodge where drinks can be purchased for the guides, and fine dining in the Big Room where kind of famous chefs prepare the day's catch to your exact breaded specification. Registered guests have complimentary use of the hot tubs that are often chuck full of local babes. Discount coupons to Buck's Bass Bliss Underwater Swimming Programs are given to frequent visitors.

An aerial view of schooling winter fishermen

An aerial view of a school of fishermen/night/all seasons

HERE'S A BRIEF SAMPLE OF WHAT YOU'LL LEARN:

✔ How to explain to the family the necessity of fishing. How to untie the moral knots of spending food-and-shoes money on new tackle. How to tie one on after you've mastered the knots. How to read a fishing tavern and determine which woman belongs to which man at different times throughout the night. How to dress like a local. How to tell when a local is lying. When to offer the warden a "gratuity." How to select the proper equipment for the type of fishing you plan and obtain a generous credit line subject to approval by an onsite personal banker. Fishing etiquette and advice on how much respect is to be paid to local customs and regulations.

✔ The two-day program runs about $795 or less per person, depending on whether you bring your child bride. The three-day program is $695 or more per person, depending entirely on your wife's double occupancy with the owner of the resort. The price includes overnight accommodations and all meals but does not include gratuities, alcohol, or "enhancement" medications.

FISHING CLUBS AND OTHER DYSFUNCTIONAL GROUPS

Hastened by the growth of a new professional class of underemployed fundraisers, the race toward organization has produced a new crop of groups dedicated to save and support a fish species. Not to be outdone by their southern cousins, the walleye fishing pros of the cold northern waters have roared into the bulrushes of modern media with yet another selection of tournaments, books, technique apparel, videos, fishing camps, and at least a minnow bucket full of opinions on how you can get more "technical."

Women's fishing groups are a more recent fancy and may be a reaction to the scantily clad scorekeepers at the all male bass tournaments. More accurately, a women's bassing group was formed soon after the lady anglers lost a New York court case in the late 1970s that protested sexual discrimination in bass tournaments. The men declared that women interfere with their privacy to pee off the side of the boat. Knowing the differences in the consumption and holding power of the two sexes, the major beer manufacturers came in a quiet court friend of the defendants.

Other new groups include:

✔ *THE KNIGHTS OF DIPTORIA,* a group of immature aquatic fly fishermen quietly encouraged by the Catholic Church. Guided by secret rituals and mood rings, the mission of the membership is to emulate anything that spends part of its life on Golden Pond, reclines on the bank of the Beaverkill, or drifts into an English chalk stream. Membership is by invitation only, sealed in a gin bottle, and floated toward you in the hush of the early morning hatch.

✔ *TOURNAMENT ANGLERS ANONYMOUS,* a support group whose members discuss their intimate feelings about more successful anglers, especially those who have their own line of plugs. Psychiatrists offer a twelve-step program that eliminates the need for a day of cheating and lying on the lake. A spouse program deals with abandonment due to the tournament circuit that forces serious anglers far from their own spawning beds. Wives deposit their eggs in mobile love nests between weigh-ins and the anglers fertilize and guard the eggs until the next big tournament purse is announced.

✔ *FLY FISHERMEN WHO FISH LIVE BAIT*, another support group that allows the sports to sleep better and have an untroubled bowel movement. Group bylaws require attendance at evening confessionals in the back of bait stores and promote member support and recovery through the mandatory "share a deep thought" hour.

SPECIAL RESORTS

Buck's "Bass Bliss" program was designed as an alternative to the dolphin swim-alongs found at tropical resorts under criticism. A dolphin's death at one of the most popular island hotel programs received considerable negative press. Further investigation showed that the fish had accidentally consumed a room service food order. Other unreported incidents surfaced during an investigation of the dolphin encounter sessions. Dolphins are good imitators. If, for example, a certain combination of water temperature, nutrients, hormones, and moon phase occurs, a female dolphin may come into heat and suggest a different interaction by bumping your crotch. Most programs do not tell you not to have sex with the dolphins, but the better schools suggest you do it on your own time.

HARASSMENT LAWS

Patterned after the hunter bill, this legislation makes interference with the lawful taking of fish during the legal season as being grounds for divorce.

The bill prohibits any conduct that would disrupt or prevent fishing activities. Prohibited conduct includes preventing trip preparation by hiding equipment, tossing worms-grubs-leeches from the refrigerator, or intentionally placing one's self between the fisherman and point of purchase. Preventing the act of fishing includes erecting barriers to deny egress from the driveway or chasing spouse on foot or with the family car, and causing the fish to flee by creating a visual, aural, olfactory, or physical stimulus. Most important is the complete ban on intentional harassment of a spouse by use of threats or actions that include interruption of normal sexual activities, preparations of favorite, timely meals, and beer butlering while watching the Bassmaster channel.

SAMPLE FISHERMAN'S PRE-NUPTIAL AGREEMENT

WHEREAS the groom has accumulated prior to marriage an invaluable supply of fishing rods, the bride waives all claims to both the joint ownership and usage of same. On specially designated occasions, the groom may allow limited use of same but no post marital rights belong to any in-laws.

WHEREAS the groom has fully disclosed to the bride-to-be the approximate present value of his fishing equipment, it is possible that something was missed, and her wedding party shall not be able to claim ownership or lease rights in a separate party agreement.

WHEREAS the groom's ability to enjoy fishing entails understanding the most current technological advances and the use of the most advanced equipment and techniques, the groom has both the right to freely dispose of older equipment to make room for the new and/or simply add property that becomes his single estate.

WHEREAS the groom will grant a special dispensation to allow the bride to handle the equipment in the normal spring housecleaning activities. It is further provided that should a fishing emergency arise, small dowry items may be pawned without advance notice until such times that the groom can concentrate on recovering same.

WHEREAS in the event of the death of the groom, the last will and testament will carry instructions that mandate the joint burial of the man and his equipment. It is further provided that the grave location is kept from the wedding party and, if necessary, a restraining order be filed against any remaining shovel-toting brothers-in-law.

Therefore and there now, in consideration of the mutual promises and agreements set forth therein and forever there more, both parties agree that any balance of taxes owed by the groom becomes a joint responsibility of the bride and her wedding party. This agreement is made in the state where the groom is a resident fisherman and shall be construed, governed, and interpreted in accordance with the laws of the Commonwealth or the Department of Fish and Game, depending on the season.

HOOKS, LINES, AND SINKERS

Just how much equipment does a fisherman need? There are no simple answers, especially if you are married and have a joint checking account. The first consideration should be what you had before you married (see Pre-Nuptial Agreement, page 67). Should starter kits or hand-me-downs be counted? Most experts at the tavern say no. The second thing to consider is based on the relationship of your annual expenditures to your net income. If your wife repeated the traditional vows of "to obey and turn over all income," your net income is the joint income of both breadwinners. The third consideration is whether you taught your wife the use of firearms.

If the terms "gross" and "net" confuse you, what the S&L loan sharks made on your account is "gross," and "net" is what your wife lets you spend once the Pampers, gas, and mascara bills are paid. Or put another way, your total salary is gross in the eye of your mother-in-law, and your net is what you'd use to hang her off the side of the boat.

Your wife will usually judge your excess by how high the stack in the corner is. A novice pile is up to four feet high, not including the rods; an adolescent pile is six feet high and not leaning; and an adult pile can go to eight feet high or to the ceiling, yet another reason to own an older house.

Buy what you absolutely need, and the final judge of that is any pre-selected group of three tackle retailers. If you are going on a guided trip, the outfitters are usually very specific about what you should take. A sample list for most fishing:

FISHING OUT OF A BOAT

Compass	Condoms	Camera	Spare tackle
Navigation chart	Clothing	Film	Spare boat plug
Extra spark plug	Landing net	Suntan lotion	Anchor
Ice chest	Fish divining stick	Binoculars	Survival suit
Beer	Spare condoms	Air mattress	American flag
More beer	Sunglasses	Portable radio	Shotgun
Soft cushion	Whistle	Bait	

FISHING ALONG A RIVER

SAME AS ABOVE
Waders
Wading stick
Flying gaff
Life preserver
Your favorite blanket
A jug of wine
More condoms
And thou

SHORE OR PIER FISHING

SAME AS ABOVE
Picnic lunch
Boom box
Harpoon with extra rope

Major purchases, such as boats, are an appropriate subject for family discussion, especially when they are not at home.

HOOKS

Fishing means catching fish, and hooks are the most important piece of equipment you can own. One of man's first tools, hooks were invented after surface-feeding fish discovered the harpoon. The first hooks were made of stone, and the poor fishing associated with this choice of materials was called the Pathetical Heavily Stoned Age (just before the Dawn of the Cave Right to Bear Arms). There is evidence that prehistoric man experimented with bone as hook materials, which would explain man's missing rib in the Bible story, but Christian scholars refuse to link this discovery to a wife's intuitive disdain for opening day ceremonies.

The New Age man started tinkering with metals out in the garage and discovered copper hooks, then later bronze hooks, then still later iron hooks, and finally, steel, all before the Christian era. Hook making became an important part of the needle industry in Europe. Modern hooks use steel as the principal material and refinements have been primarily in the shape of the bend, the angle of the barb, high-tech sharpening, and finishing treatments to protect against rust and corrosion while stuck in your ear.

✔ *THE SHANK:* Some fishermen prefer a long shank for sharp-toothed fish, but excessive leverage built into a length like that could cause an early break. Use wire leader instead.

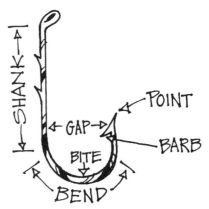

✔ *THE GAP:* Has to be wide enough to easily hook the caster's ear.

✔ *THE BEND:* The curved portion should not be too round so it bends easy and not too sharp an angle so it breaks. The bend can be more open, more closed, or standard with parallel tines.

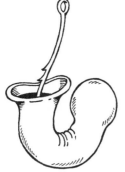

✔ *THE BITE OR THROAT:* Should be deep enough so, once hooked, the fish will slide down from the point of the barb and be firmly impaled. At this point, the fish experiences a new sense of commitment to the matters at hand.

✔ *THE BARB:* The part that refuses to "let the fish off the hook." It's easiest to set a hook that has no barb and is high fashion among catch and release fishermen and the law in special waters. When fishing for hard-mouth trophies, the barb is filed down and the point shortened. A new hook intended for "safe" fishing is intended for use on wild fish until the more disease-prone hatchery fish have all been caught.

✔ *THE POINT:* The sharp end that goes through the fish flesh first.

There are as many refinements to hooks as there are techniques and fishermen. Some hooks have added barbs along the shank to hold the bait and plastic worms better. Others have a small wire attached from the eye to the point to keep the hook relatively weed free. Most hope that the warden doesn't catch them with barbed hooks in catch and release waters.

There are two measurement systems. In one, the smallest number is ascribed to the largest hook, as in #1 largest to #32 smallest hook. The other system reverses what was just said with 1/0 being the smallest hook. It is in hook sizing system that fishing gurus have managed to make no sense at all. At the First International Conference to Set Hook Sizes, the older established Norwegian hook companies bought enough votes to pass a standard loosely based on the measurement of their children's growth. In the cool, crisp moral environment of the fjordlike setting, Norwegian elders first decided on the perfect-size child. The perfect-size girl had to have sufficient neck muscles to wear the one-hundred-pound candelabra at the Saint Lutefiska Festival, while the perfect-size boy would have hands and arms large enough to pull nets through the Swedish neighbor's fish farm. The perfect fish hook size is shown above. To get a smaller hook, stand in increments of exactly one foot farther away from this standard.

✔ *HOOK AND LINE COMBINATIONS:* Under fifteen-pound test line, use hooks smaller than 4/0. Over sixteen-pound test line, use hooks larger than 4/0 or screw it—just use whatever hooks are in the bottom of your tackle box.

LINES

Monofilament line manufacturers say that the ideal line for one type of fish or technique may not be suitable for another and have created specialty lines to meet all the demands of the sport. Top chemists have mixed polymers to engineer characteristics for different applications.

If using ultra light gear, strong lines are offered with "flexibility" and even less line memory than the caster. Other lines just have smaller diameters. For standard spinning reels, high-stress polymers resist abrasion, and in casting reels, a low line memory prevents backlash.

Lines are now treated with UV inhibitors to maintain strength and elasticity after more than twelve months in sunlight wrapped around a seabird. For high-visibility fishing, special pigments gather and retain all available light. These lines are not popular in illegal low-light fishing.

Cold-weather fishing lines are formulated for handling below-zero temperatures but cannot be used for warm weather. Condom manufacturers hoping to diversify are experimenting with a low-stretch polyester core and a flexible copolymer nylon sheath that reduces line strength but offers maximum sensitivity.

Fly-casting lines used to be made out of horsehair, and the bare-butt horses of that era had a hard time keeping the flies off. For more information, see Fly-fishing as an Art Form and Social Dysfunction.

SINKERS

Sinkers are weights used to hold your lure at a desired depth as they are dragged along the bottom with your bait floating freely behind or accidentally swallowed by the trophy lunker on the way to the tournament weigh-in. Sinkers affect the way a lure works, so experiment with different sizes and shapes in the privacy of your bathtub. Use only clean, clear water unless you are planning to fish the hydroelectric plant's backwaters. In that case, test sinkers in the tub after your mother-in-law takes her monthly sponge bath.

The most popular sinker is the split shot, a small lead sinker easily pinched shut with your fingers or teeth. The American Dental Association approves the biting of split shot when used in a conscientiously applied program of oral hygiene and regular professional care. Most bait-fishing guides have special dental insurance riders that allow for tooth replacement with a quality alloy so they can open longnecks in case everyone forgot an opener.

HOW TO RIG A SINKER

There are as many sinker shapes as there are odd-shaped fishermen—little bullets, eggs, pencils, teardrops, and torpedoes attached to a swivel and used to anchor or drift bait along the bottom. Manufacturers improve sinkers with cosmetic decorations such as plastic eyes and with rubber gaskets to minimize line damage, but you can make your own signature sinkers over the kitchen stove. When your dentist reviews your charts with quiet amusement and selects the color of his new BMW, he does not factor in the trade-in value of the old lead fillings in your mouth. During the fitting for an upper plate, demand their return.

BOBBERS

In many respects, fishing is just another irritating activity. It irritates the little lady, the boss, and your neighbors, but most of all, it irritates the fish. Bobbers are a way of measuring this irritation.

Bobbers come in all sizes and shapes. The only important feature is that the bobber floats. Sample shapes include:

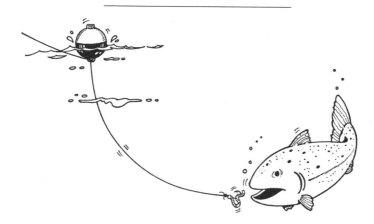

Smart fishermen will use a surface lure as a bobber. When you reel in, you just might snag a surface feeder. The latest developments include battery-operated illuminated bobbers.

BUCK'S BONUS TIP: **Shh! When no one from the local gin mill is watching, fly fishermen will attach a high hackled dry fly on a dropper above a wet fly and watch this "strike indicator" for a strike. Nobody, but nobody, dares call it a bobber.**

FISHING RODS

THE FIRST RODS: Images on limestone walls show the first fisherman using his unit as the original fishing rod. The line was carefully secured by a domestic partner. This early art explains the psychological importance of both fishing and new equipment to the modern male. It's just another dick thing.

Large fish caught by accident abruptly ended this use of early tackle. The wall markings that signify speech do not adequately express the primal screaming. Smarter fishermen who could learn from another person's mistakes tied the fishing line to a finger. A historical note of interest is that the first fly fisherman used his pinkie finger as it was the most sensitive once his mood ring was removed. Once the shoreline fish were thinned out by finger fishing, anglers needed a rod that could cast and started using the switches commonly taken to their servants and forgetful wives. The next important development in fishing rod technology came as a result of the Kennedy family going into Southeast Asia to look for scotch thinners and stumbling across bamboo poles, remarking that this fly rod material would be good enough to encourage an undeclared war. The continuing social and psychological importance of fishing rods is frequently reinforced by natural history magazines studying tribal cultures and mores.

THE LATEST RODS: Selection cannot be more confusing for the uninitiated as manufacturers spread their wares to match species and fishing techniques. Add the personality mongers and public relations experts, and the mix boils. Generally speaking, freshwater rods are lighter and saltwater rods are heavier.

As a concession to the sheer merchandising strength of the industry, Buck will describe the simpler distinctions.

✔ *SPINNING RODS:* Characterized by longer, more tubular handles and larger line guides so as not to slow the curls of the line as thrown.

✔ *CASTING RODS:* Built with a pistol-grip handle with finger holds. Other bait casting rods include pitching, flipping, and who knows what other cute phrases have popped up since the writing of this book. For that matter, buy a rod blank and some handle material and have a rod made to fit your hand, much like getting a good bowling ball.

✔ *FLY RODS:* Described in another section but it should be noted here that fly fishermen generally rely more on material selection and, while less likely to be swayed by the personality endorsements, are subject to fawning brand loyalty.

Other key considerations when selecting rods include:

✔ *LENGTH:* The longest rods are used for the longest casts, up to ten feet and beyond. Any rod from five and a half to eight feet will catch most any fish. The one you should use has less to do with specific technique or species than how much you had to fork over for it.

✔ *DIAMETER:* There is a rush to thinner and lighter rods to match the heightened sensitivities of the modern ecologically fine-tuned angler. This does not include bass tournament anglers.

✔ *MATERIALS:* Big disputes revolve around the selection of graphite or fiberglass in the manufacturing of rods. Graphite has stiffer butt sections and softer tips, while modern fiberglass rods are more uniform, with softer action along the length. Allowing the characteristics of each, the arguments support the newer technology of graphite, but in general, it's a lot like selecting the real winner at a World Federation of Wrestling match. If you are not on the lake and fishing, it's all smoke.

BUCK'S BONUS TIP: The latest merchandising trick is to separate rods by species: bass, walleye, etc. They look alike and will catch carp, bullheads, and other jetsam and flotsam with equal ease.

ASSAULT RODS: The Senatorial New Age Coalition has introduced a bill to ban the import and manufacture of "semiautomatic assault rod and reels," claiming that these pieces of equipment formerly considered sporting devices are now being used for random and wanton destruction of fish life. Included are: all rods/reels advertised using the words "powerstick," "lunkerstick," "predator," or ".38/.357 bullet reels," and certainly any foreign-made samurai mega cast stick."

The bill does not seek to ban any of the following: cane poles, branches, twigs, and sticks with string or twine attached, or any rod/reel produced before calendar year 1899.

The Coalition has already forced the passage of a weeklong waiting period for powerstick ownership and requires identification documents for purchase of all other rods and reels not specifically prohibited by local concerned citizen committees. Those who want to own or operate an assault rod will be required to fill out a form with the dealer and wait seven days while copies of the application containing all your secrets are posted on the city's telephone poles.

Fishermen have aligned with the major fishing tackle manufacturers to point out that waiting periods have not reduced bass kill on the major lakes. The Friends of Bass argue for mandatory penalties for the use of assault rods in the commission of a fishing crime. In closed testimony, the wife of the Speaker of the Southern California Legislative Assembly said, "No civilian needs a semiautomatic assault rod and reel. American society need not accommodate the heavily tackled, fast driving, and liquored up tournament boys who deal in recreational intoxicants and proclaim open warfare on bass."

REELS

Bait casting reels, which were first used in Europe during the eighteenth century, feature a spool that revolves while the line unwinds. The first imports had a gear ratio of one spool revolution for each turn of the handle. It took an American from Kentucky to make the real more useful by gearing the spool for higher ratios. The gear ratio or number of times the spool rotates to a revolution of the reel handle can be 4:1, 5:1, etc. The lower the ratio, the more power expended. The higher the ratio, the more quickly the line moves but with less power behind it.

Another innovation is the drag, a braking system that slows the line coming off the reel. Drag comes with either a star or lever control. If you turn a star drag clockwise while fishing north of the equator, the line goes out with more resistance. How much drag to use? When fishing saltwater, pros may set a strike drag position of one-quarter the breaking strength of the line. For general trolling, it may be set up to 30 percent of the total drag available. When fishing fresh water, drag is used to tire a large fish or, with the spool click flipped on, wake a fly fisherman.

Originated in England, spinning reels introduced a spool that was on the same axis as the rod. The line off a spinning reel loops (or spins) out from the spool, and since friction is reduced, longer casts and lighter lures became possible. Line is controlled with your nostril finger.

HOW LURES CATCH FISH

Color, noise, motion, and size of a lure irritate a fish into making a strike. If it's a damn hot, stinky day with fish thinking about the cooler days of fall, a good lure will bring out the worst in a fish rumble, especially if the local predators think the intruder is from a "bad" weed bed.

✔ *COLOR:* Experts behind the retail counter recommend using silver on clear days and in shallow water; silver/blue in deep, clear water; gold on dark days and in dark water; gold and red fluorescent in muddy water; silver fluorescent and chartreuse in dark, deep water; the reverse of the above, whatever is on sale, or, if the clerk cut your credit card in two as instructed by MasterCard, whatever is in your tackle box.

✔ *NOISE:* Fish are irritated by any interruption of their quiet world, particularly in the spawning beds where the little ones are sleeping. As anyone who has a colicky newborn knows, any noise upsets the parent equally which makes for really good fishing.

✔ *MOTION:* The lateral line of a fish alerts the fish pea brain whenever a predator or baitfish is moving close. If either has an unnatural motion, predator instincts react and the lure hooks better be screwed in tight. Bait-casting plugs sold at Buck's Bass Resort imitate the

social behavior of the fisherman. The familiar rocking motion of the popper called the "Porker" is a surefire bass buster on Big Babe Lake.

✔ *SIZE:* For reasons of ego alone, big fish eat big fish and the sizing works downward. If the preferred foods are not available, a fish will eat as much as possible of as many as possible as soon as possible and as often as possible, and during these times it doesn't make any difference to the fish what you're using. Most fishermen never have this experience.

ARTIFICIAL LURES

BAIT-CASTING LURES:

✔ *SPINNERS:* The sound, the flash, and the colors of a spinner excite a predator as quickly and completely as heavy metal excites that teenage thug up in his room. Spinner blades can be attached to wire, surrounded by bangles, beads, and short skirts and used for both trolling and casting.

✔ *THE NEXT DECISION IS TO CHOOSE BETWEEN:*

AN IN-LINE SPINNER

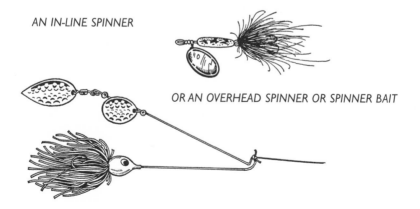

OR AN OVERHEAD SPINNER OR SPINNER BAIT

✔ *SPOONS:* The use of spoons has been documented by the flatware industry as being started by some bumbler dropping a soup spoon in the water and having it hit by a hungry undercooked fish. There are better stories elsewhere but this one is a good explanation of why your wife won't let you near her good silver. Spoons come in different sizes, shapes, and colors. A spoon that works particularly well in the Rio Grande is a U.S. Customs badge with a hook on it.

✔ *PLUGS:* Surface plugs are designed to imitate a troubled fish or natural bait. A favorite is the popper, a lure with a concave face that tips up when it floats, dragging its rear down in the water. The popping occurs when the lure is jerked horizontally, scooping and "popping" the water. Any floating lure that resembles food to a predator fish can be successfully jerked across the water.

✔ *RAPALAS:* A popular line of lures designed to recreate the twitch, quiver, and wobble of a wounded minnow. Still hand carved, these rugged wood originals have earned a reputation for catching all fish under all conditions. Imitators are crippling minnows in fish labs to discover any fish infirmity Rapala may have missed.

✔ *FLOATING/DIVING LURES:* Equipped with fixed or adjustable diving "lips" that enable the lure to dive deep while being retrieved. Larger lipped lures are currently held in high esteem in the sparkling waters near Hollywood and Vine. Lipless sinking lures are weighted to sink at a certain rate.

✔ *SUNKEN LURES:* Best known as jigs—hooks with a lead head, painted bright, and best rigged with a minnow dressed in a grass skirt. Jigs have probably caught more fish than any other lure in the history of modern fishing, but the big lure tackle industry doesn't want you to know this.

ARTIFICIAL BAIT

The first rubber worm patent was issued in 1877. Once new synthetics like polyvinyl chloride were put to use, the niche makers created an explosion of colors and shapes. Product manufacturers started to cover, then fortify the new worms with flavors and scents. The outer layers of the first lures contained salt in an effort to preseason the catch. Now there are worms that are "cooked in Hawg Scents" and garlic-flavored worms for the Italian market. Another manufacturer is experimenting with MSG as an ingredient for the growing Chinese fishing population.

The American Rubber Institute is suppressing stories that old-fashioned lures work best, especially the live baits. The world-record brown trout, weighing over thirty-eight pounds, was caught on a hook baited with corn and marshmallows, and it's rumored that the marshmallows were a generic brand.

REAL BAIT

✔ *CORN:* A piece of corn recently took a state-record rainbow in North Carolina. Lure manufacturers are saying it was snagged illegally. Corn growers contend it proves the need for more ethanol.

✔ *CRAYFISH:* These are the best live bait in rivers and creeks but are more expensive and are good as lunch. Remove pincers and hook in tail section as they normally swim backwards. Or just throw in a pot of boiling water with Zatarain's Crab Boil.

✔ *DOUGH BALLS, CHEESE BALLS, STINKBALLS:* A natural bait for carp and catfish you can make when Mom isn't home. Mix flour, cornmeal, and anything to flavor. Bring to boil in cheesecloth and cook until they float. Carp like them sweet. Catfish like them stinky.

✔ *EGGS:* Fresh salmon spawn are good as a late-night snack or in cheesecloth, a boffo bottom bait.

✔ *FROGS AND SALAMANDERS:* Found in swampy areas and hooked through both lips with a #2 or #4 hook are certified bass killers unless first caught by French "frog" restaurateurs and covered with a horrid sauce.

✔ *GRASSHOPPERS:* The traditional scourge of the prairie grain farmer and an effective bait for many freshwater game fish. Catch by hand or swat with a folded paper or flyswatter, which stuns them enough to be put in a jar. Hook through mouth and out belly or tie on live with a rubber band.

✔ *LEECHES:* An excellent bait for walleyes and can be bought in most bait shops. When Buck was in Vietnam operating his own M.A.S.H. unit, he collected leeches in rice paddies just by wearing loose clothing. You don't have to join the army to find leeches, as any good brackish water will do. Roll up your pant legs or, better yet, wear shorts, and stand barefoot until you've collected enough bait for the weekend. It's more comfortable to take the bait off your legs and put them in a jar than to let them ride to the fishing hole with you, though the longer they stay attached, the larger they become.

✔ *LUNCHEON MEAT:* Good, processed pork shoulder is too tasty to throw to the fish. The gel, however, will keep your ferrules from sticking. Whatever ferrules are.

✔ *MINNOWS:* These little fish are known as baitfish to the initiated. They can be bought by the dozen in bait shops but you have to bring your own container or take your chances on getting an oily Styrofoam chest that the owner just drained his car oil from. Bait through lips, under the dorsal fin, or thread hook with point coming out butt. Hook in the tail if you want baitfish to see where it's been trolling.

BUCK'S BONUS TIP: Since fish hale minnows head first, two headed minnows, commonly found in the circus, work best.

✔ *PORK RIND:* The first strip bait. The pork-shaped frog is the most popular pattern, followed by eels and split tails. Packaged, these also make a great Superbowl snack.

✔ *WORMS:* Perhaps the first bait and found almost everywhere, but mostly under things. A conservative estimate is fifty thousand worms per acre, especially if it's an acre where your neighbor's dog lives. If the dog lives with a Swedish family with a healthy appetite of lutefisk, the count can go as high as five hundred thousand per acre.

BUCK'S BONUS TIP: Think free bait before you worm your dog or fishing partner.

If none of the above works, most tournament fishermen just shoot the damn things. Any large caliber handgun works. Caution: Shoot at a right angle to the water's surface and watch for snorkels. And wardens for that matter.

BOATS

THE THEORY OF THE BLACK HOLE: Boats are fisherman containers, and those containers come in all sizes and shapes. The first boat was built to get away from the crowded shoreline. Every boat built since was to get away from the wife and kids.

Boat manufacturers piece together materials for bankers to underfinance. Bankers set interest rates and payment schedules by how often they can use the vessel. You can normally shave a fraction off the interest rate if you stock fresh bait on their preferred weekends.

✔ *BASS BOATS:* Built for the tournament fisherman. Remote, foot-control steering so solo fisherman can arrive at the dock holding the trophy with both hands. Used to run moonshine and outrun revenuers. Extra-high sides for decal display. A locked live well to hide the standby lunker should the tournament waters not be friendly. The new boats have options like sonar busters that drop tinfoil shards in the paths of competitors' depth finders.

 BUCK'S BONUS TIP: If you catch a trophy walleye from your new bass boat, your warranty may be voided.

✔ *CANOES:* For those of us who grew up in scout canoes, this boat is an all-purpose small vessel for easy waters. The canoe is particularly good in the weeds of bass lakes and can be poled with little difficulty. Outfitted with a small electric or gasoline motor on a square stern, a canoe is used on many of the flatter, calmer freshwater lakes and rivers. The chief advantages of canoes are that they can be cheap, are easier to carry and portage than other vessels, and are considered more "native" than powerboats.

✔ *FOLDING BOATS:* Folding boats won't sink with mother-in-law during a flash thunderstorm and you underneath trying to tip it over. When collapsed, it doesn't always look like a boat so your wife won't know if you bought one or not.

✔ *INFLATABLE BOATS:* Easier for the little woman to carry. It's a smart move to have floorboards put in as these boats usually leak enough to keep your live minnows fresh in the bottom of the boat. A great boat if you have a neighbor who pesters you into taking him along. Have that fat windbag blow up the boat.

✔ *JOHNBOATS:* The original boat had wood planks that swelled and the name came from "Oh, that's John's boat!" John almost sold his boat to Ralph, which was already a name for a party boat puker.

✔ *ROWBOATS (OR UTILITY BOATS):* Found all over Minnesota and other Midwestern states, rowboats are made of wood or aluminum, have gunnels full of spiders, wood that needs scraping, or aluminum rivets that need replacing. Many the back of a leg has been fried on the aluminum seat of a rowboat. Except while in season, these boats lay like beached whales along the lake's edge. Considered the first training boat, the rowboat comes with oars that bend, loose oarlocks, chunks of rope tied to a coffee can of cement, and a bottom littered with dried-up angleworms and hooks lying in wait for the first bare foot. A motor can be a boon or bane, depending how sturdy the transom is. The first young owner will paint his or her name first and then the rest of the boat if there is any paint left over. Rowboats are the summer equivalent to secondhand snowmobiles in the Midwest—cheap, low maintenance, and not considered an asset by your loan officer.

✔ *WALLEYE BOATS:* Northern entrepreneurs saw how successful bass boats were and decided to capitalize on yet another popular species. Walleye boats have deep V-shaped hulls and high sides for larger bodies of open water and Swedish baby boomers. Several models have one side higher so you don't have to show anyone your meager stringer.

BOAT ACCESSORIES

✔ *ANCHORS:* Boat anchors are an important dredging device for the Minnesota Department of Natural Resources. Any advantage of being able to sit in the front of the boat was lessened by the responsibilities of handling the anchor. Duties start with a big splash, followed by a pull on young muscles as the weight slips into the darkness carefully so no fish is bonked on the anchor's way down to the bottom. If you're an old anchor-hand, you'll have tied knots in the rope at ten-foot intervals so you'll know how deep to fish bottom fish. If the anchor hits hard, it's good walleye bottom. If it hits soft, it's the local snorkeling club.

✔ *BAIT BOXES:* Minnow buckets can be double metal pails, one inside the other like a Ukrainian egg, or just cheap Styrofoam containers. The advantage of the first is that tied off the side of the boat, the fish that you are throwing spoons at can sneak up and find out from the bait minnows how they are being treated and whether you practice catch and release.

✔ *GAFFS:* There are two principal types—the straight gaff and the flying gaff. Smart captains will hook up a rope to the straight gaff and tie the bitter end to the fighting chair. Gaffs are used to hook a big fish into the boat so you can shoot it with a shotgun.

✔ *MOTORS:* Recreational items with high retail and low resale values, much like an ex-wife. In the early, innocent days of fishing, boats came first, then the largest motor possible. The thought wasn't to balance the two into a smoothly functioning unit, the point was to go as fast as you could without ripping the transom off. The other improvements include power steering, power trim, and quiet exhaust systems so you don't wake up the fish rights activist.

The new gasoline powered outboard engines are smaller, quieter, and more powerful. Four cycle motors deliver less fuel consumption, produce no oil smoke, and run as quiet as a Japanese outboard motor factory after a nationalist fervor break.

Electric motors were originally designed for quiet running under the noses of pesky game wardens. Powered by a twelve-volt battery, these small motors are mounted near a "main" motor and best used to slip into fish farms and test spawning beds.

Regardless of what your mother-in-law says, the question of how many motors to own is not an appropriate family table topic.

✔ *NAMES:* While it may seem silly to consider the name of the boat as an accessory, think how silly many fly fishermen are in adopting the III, Colonel, Ret., and Esquire. You'd be shocked if you knew some of the pet names used for their overpriced cane poles.

✔ *NETS:* It's handy to have a net to hang beer over the side and to catch turtles should the fishing get slow. If you happen to net a really unhappy snapping turtle, pass the entire mess back to Dad.

✔ *OARS:* Oars are used to move a boat, imitate a beaver, or for as simple a task as pushing a younger brother out of the boat.

✔ *PERSONAL FLOTATION DEVICE (PFD):* Life vests were created by the apparel industry. Despite the captain's orders, large women's breasts are not considered PFDs by the United States Coast Guard.

✔ *STRINGERS:* Can be as simple as a rope, string, shoelaces, or sticks or as complicated as metal wire clamps that hook and lock the jaw of the fish to a wire rope. Do you lift the stringer while trolling or racing back to shore? Think about this. If your stringer has only small pan fish, they rarely have a chance to go this fast. If your stringer is jammed with lunkers, make sure the knot is tightly tied and teach those predators a lesson.

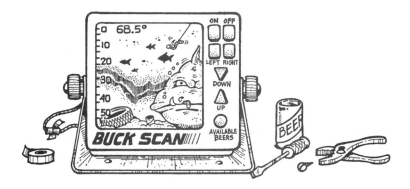

FISHFINDERS

Fish finder manufacturers are selling machines that include zoom images, fish and bottom alarms, digital depth readouts, high-definition display, TiVo for NASCAR updates, text messaging from game and fish officers watching you through spotting scopes. With a full swivel mount, the sounders can be turned skyward for wild fowl migrations, and the latest models include radar detection to sweep the lakeshore for a badge crawling up on your honey hole.

Once you have the equipment that tells you all about where you are, you'll not only want to return to that same spot but, in deep salt water, find a way home. If you don't like technology in general, mark your spot with a float, tie a scarf to the shoreline, pull the boat-girl's pants down for a look-see and possible digital exam, pile rocks alongside the stream, draw an arrow in the sand, or if you have an old salt water boat, just follow your oil slick back to the dock. The old surefire way was to triangulate back to the dock.

You can also yell at an occupied dock, follow a particular shore light, or aim at any flashing neon sign advertising a liquid product that goes good with beernuts.

✔ *THE LORAN METHOD:* In use since World War II and is an acronym for Long Range Navigator. The system uses powerful low-frequency radio transmitters and sensitive receivers. Transmitter stations and chains are located all over the world. M designates a master stations; secondary or slave stations may tell you where you are; only your mother-in-law can be counted on to tell you exactly where to go. The M or master station transmits at precise time intervals (group repetition intervals or GRI) and the slave stations transmit at other exact intervals following the master. The Loran receiver measures the time difference (TD) between the master and two slave impulses and plots your location, shows up as a line of positioning (LOP) crossing on a screen.

You can measure Loran by three indexes—absolute accuracy, reasonable accuracy, and navigator error. The first allows only 0.1 to 0.25 nautical miles error, reasonable accuracy puts you within two thousand feet, and a bad navigator should be set just offshore, remaining within lights of the village.

✔ *THE GPS METHOD (OR GLOBAL POSITIONING SYSTEM):* The system is capable of finding even those fishermen with multiple personalities, which includes most commercial fishermen. U.S. Department of Defense satellites used in the system will not only show longitude and latitude but also altitude and time—worldwide. Since the absolute position of the satellite is known, a receiver measures the relationship between satellite and boat via radio signals. Three different satellites yield a surface fix. Once fixed, our nation's spy agencies can dial into your illegal and likely immoral activities.

✔ *THE BUCKSTER METHOD:* One you get your GPS receiver, interface it with your auto route finder to plot the course for picking up your buddies on the way to the lake and map out the lake according to your fishing needs: beer, bait, and babes.

GENERAL FISHING TECHNIQUES

FLY-FISHING VERSUS BAIT CASTING

In the interest of bringing the two philosophies of technique together, Buck has interviewed personalities from both sides of the riverbank and carefully reports their positions.

WHY FLY-FISH?: With their attention to detail, fly fishermen catch only the fish they want to catch, leaving rough fish to bait-fishermen. Fly-fishing is a solitary sport that does not have to be shared and is thus codependent-free. In an age of instant gratification, however, learning this discipline can take years. In an age of generalists, fly-fishing allows you to become a specialist on a subject that interests only a small part of the population and even they think you aren't that interesting. Fly-fishing purists breathe life into a dead language, Latin, which enhances their standing in the Knights of Columbo. Idle chitchat is avoided by concentrating on the specific benefits of a certain hatch or condition, which will shut down your social calendar and let you fish even more. If you are a died-in-the-wool catch and release activist, remote lodge owners and equally remote masters of the art form will welcome you into a world filled with warmed Cognac and hand-rolled cigars. Fly-fishing marine biologists are discussing such issues as whether bait casting is a birth defect and whether women who bear tournament fishermen should be sterilized. The more open-minded gear guys allow that fly-fishing may be a response to high density urban living rather than a genetic trait and that with proper counseling, a fly fisherman would rather leave all that paraphernalia behind.

WHY BAIT AND SPIN CAST?: Unlike fly fishermen whose existential goal is to think like a fish, bait fishermen only want to fun with the fish. Cranker ranks are growing because it's cheaper, less complicated, and much more fun. And because they can do it in T-shirts and Levis. And drink full-bodied beer out of longneck bottles and not worry about the deposits. And smoke cheap crooked cigars that have been soaked in rum. And get the big-busted farm girls.

GENERAL FISHING

Classic signs and symptoms of fishermen in the months prior to opening day:
- ✔ Loss of interest in all activities not connected with fishing
- ✔ Systemic anxiety
- ✔ Early morning waking
- ✔ Painful bowel movements
- ✔ Thoughts of death

✔ Difficulty in concentration

✔ Irritability

✔ Incessant, uncontrollable crying

One week prior to opening day and following one trip to the tackle shop:

✔ Excessive elation

✔ Exaggerated belief in one's abilities

✔ Increased activity, including sex, with or without a partner

✔ Impulsive buying without regard to checkbook balance

✔ Less need for sleep

✔ Frequent urination, spitting

Opening day:

✔ Not available for comment—gone fishing

Closing day:

✔ Depending on success, feelings of hopelessness and worthlessness

✔ See above months prior to opening day

READING THE WATERS

Reading the waters is a euphemism for deciding in your own mind where the fish might be hanging out. There are two viewing platforms: The overview observations of surface habitat and the underview prognostications of what truly lies below the water's surface.

Overviews are tempered with advice from guides, first and second wives, gas station attendants, and dockside kibitzers. Superstition, folktales, and other mental maladies are compared with topographic maps. Overviews of saltwater fishing prospects are as simple as the identification of riptides and variations in water color, the oily stink of feeding bluefish, and the spotting of bait feeders such as frigate birds, terns, gannets, and pelicans. A sure sign of game fish is a flock of gulls hanging around the back of a successful sport fishing boat, and you best get over there quick. Tip: Schools of fishermen are the best indication of good fishing or a nude beach.

Underviews are what the fish see. Short of getting into a wet suit, anglers can use the new electronic technology to identify good fishing habitat, or draw conclusions from the overviews. Saltwater fishermen work ledges, shelves, and ridges that concentrate baitfish and baitfish eaters and catch and release any sport divers in the area. Ordinary freshwater fishermen are just so happy to be away from those goofball relatives on the dock that they really don't care what equipment they brought with them. Tournament anglers and manufacturers have coined the word "structure" to identify where fish like to hang out and browbeat any available set of ears with structure-related nonsense to sell fishing "systems." They have also created an optical industry by recommending polarizing lenses to allow a clearer look at the river bottom. If you reverse the lenses, the fish can see you better too.

READING WATERS BY TYPE:

✔ *LAKES:* Buck provides an aerial view of his private Big Babe Lake in northern Minnesota to illustrate the more salient features of lake fish habitat.

Once the season opens, fish move into the most comfortable, weed-infested, timber-jammed shallows they can find. If cooler water is important, they'll move along the edge of the first drop-off, just like an enemy submarine.

✔ *OCEANS:* Ask the local surf fishermen if the ocean is open for fishing that day and, in appreciation, wish them enough good fortune that they can someday afford to go out fishing on a boat like yours.

✔ *STREAMS:* These waters come in all sizes and shapes, deep and shallow, fast and slow, some with banks sloped for easy beaching. Bottoms can be rocky and harbor important trout bait or covered with enough quicksandlike mud to hold your hip boots tight until the grizzlies start their night feeding.

Fish are lazy and will lay, with mouths pointed upstream, to dine. They'll float downstream of rocks, in holes, in riverbank undercuts, and in any curve where the current is slowed. Species have their own agendas for selecting their rivers. The larger, slower bass find it more difficult to hold in the fast-moving water where a trout actively and easily feeds. If the bass is a lot larger than the smart-aleck trout, the fish-eat-fish brutality of Mom Nature reappears.

OTHER RECOMMENDED READINGS:

✔ *READING THE TEMPERATURE OF THE WATER:* Fish have a preferred temperature and single-mindedly seek that comfortable environment. A change in the temperature can trigger a migration or stimulate activities such as spawning. The thermocline is the middle layer of water in a lake where the temperature changes quickest and where freshwater fish hang the longest. Big saltwater game fish will leave preferred their waters when food becomes scarce or when they can hear more than one tournament boat. If you are fishing the most chemically polluted waters, the mercury poisoning level will register along the lateral lines. If the redness rises above the lateral line, the water is too hot, except in Canadian waters where metric measurements make the readings meaningless.

✔ *READING THE PH OF THE WATER:* Use a pH meter to find the chemical optimum or pH break line and place lures just above it. The primary break line shows the biggest change in the pH, and 7.2 to 8.8 is the best environment to catch fish. In water over 9.0 or under 7.0, fish are less aggressive and hard to catch. Way over 9.0 and you won't need to pickle them later.

✔ *READING THE CLARITY OF THE WATER:* By measuring light intensity, you can select the lure color and type for each species. Commercial color selectors are available, offering up yet another mock science from the artificial lure manufacturers.

HOW TO BAIT YOUR HOOK

You should have already figured out how to bait your own hook, but Buck makes this book even more user-friendly.

Hook rigs are used to weight the lure into place yet allow the hooked bait to move naturally. A simple surface rig is a split shot above the live bait on a line topped with a bobber. Two popular rigs are the Texas and Carolina. The Texas rig has a bullet-shaped weight at the tip and an angled hook that puts the tip of the point inside the worm so as not to frighten the Chicano cats swimming below the surface of the Rio Grande. The Carolina bottom-fishing rig has a small bullet weight attached to a barrel swivel that is followed by twenty to thirty inches of leader or line to a worm.

SINGLE HOOKS

✔ *FROGS:* Hook through lips or through leg. Unless you had the legs for lunch, which will adversely affect the frog's natural motion.

✔ *GRUBS, MAGGOTS:* Hook through lips. Wherever they are. Or just have Dad do it.

✔ *MINNOWS:* Hook through lips, through mouth, and out bottom of belly like night crawlers, or under dorsal fin near tail or through back. For casting, run a line through the mouth, out the gills, and hook through the back.

✔ *PLASTIC WORMS:* Buy the complete outfit with hooks included, otherwise run the hook so the eye comes out the head and the point sticks out below.

✔ *REAL WORMS:* Hook night crawlers through the tougher collar first. Loosely hook red worms back and forth along the entire shank, covering the point with the last piece. Don't lick fingers.

CHUMMING OR HOW TO BAIT THE WATER, TOO

Once you've rigged your line with the freshest of baits, shoreline odds makers look favorably on extra efforts to attract fish. While purists may fuss and object, a surefire technique is to "chum" or salt the water with even more bait in order to attract the entire school of fish.

Chumming is done to scent the water, not feed the fish. This technique works in both freshwater and saltwater, for blues in Chesapeake Bay to bluegills in Lake Labrador. Chum is nothing but fish guts and can be bought commercially frozen in bags or blocks or gathered informally from your fishing buddies. Surprisingly, fish guts are not cheap, particularly midseason, but a few southern friends have reported lower prices when purchased with food stamps.

If at all possible, keep the chum cold. Once the bag warms up, the contents will smell like your mother-in-law's pantyhose. Either scoop and throw or pour the guts into the water, but throw enough for the fish to see or smell. If the night swills equal the day swells, recycled pizza, black cigar, and stale beer chum will complete the presentation.

Saltwater captains will put chum in mesh bags, and if you can use fresh-cut bait, all the smellier. If you throw chunks of chum in the water, do it one at a time and evenly. If the fish seem to like only the chunks, it may be good enough for your mother-in-law to eat so pull anchor and head home.

Freshwater chumming requires smaller portions as the water is generally cleaner. For bluegills, perforate and hang a can of dog food over the water. Once the flies turn to maggots and start dropping, you'll have a "honey hole." In the Seattle suburb of Ballard, Scandinavians that have lazed about Snooze Boulevard dreaming of winning the Lutefisk Lottery and angling for a loose migrating salmon, have spit so much tobacco in the water that perforated snooze cans with a hook are all that's needed to jog the genetic memory of a returning hooknose.

If you have a brother-in-law, personal chumming is effective but not if you are wearing waders. While upstream, nature's porta-potty system is always open, and with little effort, you can create an acid rain condition in the fishing hole he's standing in downstream.

THE MOST IMPORTANT FISHERMAN'S KNOTS

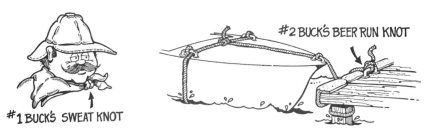

#1 BUCK'S SWEAT KNOT

#2 BUCK'S BEER RUN KNOT

#3 BUCK'S BEER KNOT

#4 BUCK'S IN-LAW SLIPKNOT

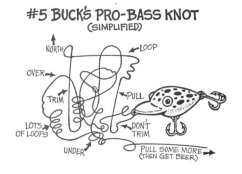

#5 BUCK'S PRO-BASS KNOT (SIMPLIFIED)

NORTH
OVER
TRIM
LOTS OF LOOPS
UNDER
LOOP
PULL
DON'T TRIM
PULL SOME MORE (THEN GET BEER)

SIX KNOTS FOR FLY-FISHING: Like everything else, fly fishermen need two more knots than necessary. Quickly, it goes like this: The backing is connected to the reel (slipknot), the hip bone is connected to the shoulder bone (oops), the fly line is connected to the leader (nail knot), the leader is connected to the tippet (blood knot), and that's the way of the Lord. Dem flies, dem flies, dem dry flies. ♪♪♪

✔ *ALBRIGHT KNOT:* Reverse spider hitch. Best tied with a mirror. Or reflection off a chalk stream.

✔ *BIMINI TWIST:* A double-line knot used for offshore trolling or making a "shock" tippet. Double end of line four feet and twist twenty times, pull ends to tighten. Wind back end tightly and make overhand knot around side of loop. Repeat on other side of loop. Wind line end three times around midlarge loop and pull end through small loop just made. Pull line and large loop tight. Add two shots of tequila for a Jiminy Bimini Twist.

✔ *BLOOD KNOT:* Ancient ceremony knot that ties two fly fishermen to a promise not to tell bass fishermen how little fun they are really having, usually between two fly-fishing leaders of different moral strengths, a father/ son relationship in many cases.

✔ *DOUBLE-LOOP CLINCH KNOT:* Used to attach a fly to a shock leader. It's a cinch. Just try it. Thatta boy.

✔ *NAIL KNOT:* For joining fly line and leader butt, this knot is used by fisher-men who can't get the hang of other knots. Just do slightly different from Bimini twist.

✔ *SPIDER HITCH:* Similar in purpose to the Bimini but quicker to tie and easier with only one intoxicated person. Wrap double line five times around thumb and pass large loop through small reverse loop, loopedy, loop. Hold it, my finger is in there. Now, pull tight.

CASTING

Unless you are fishing with explosives, you have to go to the fish by casting. To become proficient, practice in the privacy of your own cul-de-sac. Simply attach a lead sinker to a swivel at the end of your line and throw it down the street, avoiding telephone lines, neighborhood cars, and the new kids on the block. If the sinker isn't too heavy, have your little woman play catch. This exercise will help build her reflexes. Once you're able to cast into a neighbor's open car window, you've earned a beer or six.

Casting into the water is even easier since there is nothing out there to break like a closed car window. As you've learned earlier, spin-casting reels move the line from an immobile spool and your individual grip is what makes this tackle sing. Closed-face bait-casting reels are the simplest to work. All you do is push down the button, wind up, and whip the rod forward, throwing the line as you release it somewhere around 10:00 or 11:00 A.M. If you let the button go any earlier than that, you'll be pushing the breakfast hour and the eggs aren't ready yet. Once your lure goes as far as the casting gods have deemed, your reel will click back into retrieve and you are all set.

✔ *IN BAIT CASTING:* Put your lure where the fish can see and be activated by its motion, color, scent, or retail price.

✔ *IN OPEN WATER:* It's easy. Just do it. Avoid snorkle tubes.

✔ *IN TREE-FILLED PONDS:* Cast over the log and jiggle the line as you prepare to set the hook in the third limb.

✔ *ALONG THE SHORELINE:* Cast just short of the weeds and bounce the lure back toward you.

✔ *IN A CROWDED OPENING DAY:* In a few southern states, when cast sidearm, bouncing your lures off a Yankee's fishing boat is allowed, particularly if it's sitting on top of your honey hole.

 BUCK'S BONUS TIP: When fishing a crowded riverbank, cast sideways using both hands, left then right, unless you are fishing south of the equator. Yell "Fore!"

Casting tournaments are available to stretch the limits of both equipment and men, with records set annually. Some casters do well with a fifty-eight-foot throw, others an eighty-eight-foot. The record for the longest cast in the United States is over seven hundred feet. In Hollywood, casting couches are available for young women learning the sport.

HOW TO SET THE HOOK

There are three commonly accepted ways to set the hook:

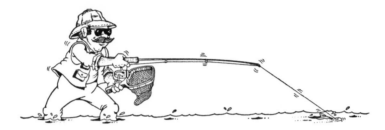

1. With the line tight, face rod toward lure and hold on while the fish sets the hook itself as it tries to run away. This method may get you "off the hook" with fish rights advocates. Maybe not.

2. Soft set. Keeping your finger tight on the line, lift the rod to a ninety degree angle from the water, slowly pulling the sharpened meat hook through the fish's tender, sensitive lips.

3. Hard set. Jerk the rod 180 degrees opposite the fish and run to the end of the boat or dock. This will not only show the fish who is boss but may boat or beach it at the same time. The southern version of this set is to beach the boat.

Variables involved in these methods include the weight of line used and the drag of reel. In meat fishing, the line is never too heavy. If the drag is not set tight or you don't have a firm hand on the spool, your set will not happen no matter how loud you curse. Play the pea-brained fish until it acknowledges your superior skill and gives up.

HOW A FISH IS HOOKED

Your hooking techniques have a lot to do with how much fight the fish will give you and the odds of a successful catch and release. If you allow the fish too much time to play with the bait or have offered too realistic an imitation, they will skip nibbling and, if from a large family, will gulp and swallow the offering.

This fish will give a short gut-wrenching fight. If you shorten the hook-up time, the hook may drift back into the gills.

The fish will come in sideways, bleed all over your new trophy jumpsuit, and die regardless of your CPR efforts.

If you hook the fish just as you feel the first bump, the point will pierce the lip and the fish will swim peacefully to you and all will be well in the fish kingdom until you screw up the release.

DOWNRIGGING

In addition to using weights, sinkers, or a weighted lure, one of the most popular ways to get your presentation to the fish is to use a downrigger as you troll from your boat. This principle is to drop a lead ball to the desired level and attach a line via a quick release. When a fish hits your lure, the line breaks away from the ball and you are free to lose the fish any way you want.

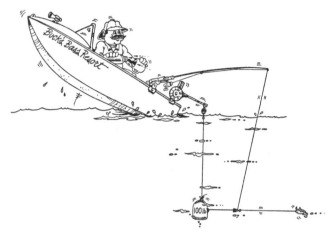

Downriggers come in both manual and electric versions. They include a slip clutch so you can set for light tension should you snag the bottom or, if fishing in the Great Lakes, a Canadian submarine. Choices vary depending on the presumed size of your balls. As most high school coaches know, balls come in all sizes and shapes. The only requirement is they hang directly below the boat. If you use a downrigger in proper British waters, a proper question is whether they hang to the right or left of the boat.

 BUCK'S BONUS TIP: When fishing downriggers near a city park, remember divers usually come in pairs and carry spear guns.

HOW TO RETRIEVE A FISH

If fishing cold water with little success, adjust the speed of your lure to the slower fish metabolism. Reel three to four cranks and let the lure sit or sink before cranking again. If your lure is nearing another boat's stringer, snag that big northern tied to the gunnel. If you hook another fisherman's line, courtesy dictates an acknowledgement of your error, and if they are bigger than you and/or their boat is faster than yours, allow them to reel in first. If not, keep cranking.

If fishing warm water, fish need a little excitement. Reel in the line more erratically. Make your lure twitch by jerking the rod left and right. As in all techniques, big twitches catch big fish. Full-body twitching by the fisherman himself sends a special message to the lunkers below and the undercover wardens in the next boat. If you get bored, write your name in the water with the tip as you reel in until the lure hits rod guide.

When you play a fish, the fish doesn't consider it play. No matter what your intentions, a fish is forced to leave its home under duress and, with the exception of many catch and release fish, their only reaction is to fight that suggestion. Most fish muscle is rich in stored sugar energy, and the big muscles are used to fight or run. In a fight with a two-hundred-pounder, a fish switches to these "afterburners," which quickly convert its glycogen into lactic acid. With just a small blood supply to rinse away the acid, fish are literally eaten from the inside. If caught and released, they become an easy snack for bears, seals, and eagles. The fashionable rush to use ultra light gear and endlessly play a fish should be accompanied with complete CPR instructions.

If you "horse" a fish with gear too large for the species, it's easier on the fish, particularly if you hydroplane them across the surface. Fish biologists report that the fish might even experience an elementary sort of glee during this quick retrieve.

When a big fish strikes a rod held by a good-looking, large woman, it's considered old-world gentlemanliness to support her efforts physically by grabbing from behind in any place that under normal circumstances may demand an apology and hold her tight until she boats the trophy. On all-woman boats, "fish-on" behavior is similar to that of first labor—fisherwomen are allowed, even encouraged to scream their innermost thoughts, especially about the men who put them in those conditions.

If you are fishing in deep salt water and have a fish on, you may bring the fish up faster than it can equalize the pressure in its air bag, sort of like the bends. There are reports of fish actually exploding on the way to the deck, which can be a great way to wake up that side of the boat. It's also one less fish to clean. If you want to release one of these deep-sea monsters, the officially recommended way to deflate the gas bladder is to chip off a scale under the tip of the pectoral fin and insert the point of a fourteen-guage hypodermic needle through the body wall. Compress sides as necessary to get fish back to normal size, withdraw needle, and place fish back in water. If you are fishing off the New Jersey shoreline, it's not hard to find large hypodermic needles. They are floating offshore downwind of the mental hospitals.

HOW TO RELEASE A FISH

It's hard to imagine the psychological and physical stress a fish undergoes as it is brought into the boat. First of all, it is not happy being pulled away from family and friends. More important, the fish is seriously not happy being caught by you of all people.

If possible, always leave the fish in the water. With a polarizing lens, you can take a picture of the fish, or hang the bait boy over the side with your new underwater camera. If it is not possible, return fish to water quickly. The big secret is that tournament fish kept in aerated live wells don't last long even though the fish has a vested interest in making a good showing. Any amount of time out of the original water harms the fish.

Minimize handling of the fish. Fish need their slime so do not wear gloves or use a cloth to pick them up. If it's that bothersome, wipe the slime on the bait boy's or guide's jacket. The brochure said the trip was all-inclusive. During the photo session, don't squeeze the fish behind the gills to give it a more menacing appearance. Unless you are fishing carp.

Don't squeeze the size of fish too hard. Fish are not ticklish and will not smile. If you are trying to squeeze out eggs, squeeze carefully and repeat softly, "I need thee more than you do." If it's a big-bellied pregnant female, lift her tender bottom with your hand and extend all the respect you normally would to a lady in her condition.

HOW TO LIFT A FISH OUT OF THE WATER: If you use a net, use one of the newer, softer cotton types with a flat bottom so the fish can lay more comfortably and with a finer mesh so as not to hook on fins. Fish are best grabbed by the tail or under the jaw. Old-timers fishing for northerns pick the snakes up by their eye sockets. Since catch and release has infiltrated their ranks, the near-blind predators bump their way through weeds and baitfish, hoping for a German dogfish to lead them across major current intersections.

HOW TO PUT BACK IN THE WATER: Lower carefully and slip the fish into the water facing the current. It's important for the fish to have fresh water going through its nose. Don't move a salmon, or any other fish, back and forth, to and fro. Have you ever seen a fish swim backwards? Have you ever thrown up through your nose?

If you've caught the dreaded bycatch and are willing to violate their fish rights, any bullhead can be caught and released by slamming your cane pole against the water, slapping the fish loose. If you do this, the other ugly fish will take it as a warning to leave your bait alone.

CATCH AND RELEASE

In earlier, simpler times, catch and release was an accident. Now, like everything else, it's done on purpose.

In times of limited supplies, catch and release keeps our atavistic souls alive, at once proving that the finned quarry can be conquered, and yet preserving our purity of soul by granting continued life. Catch and release is, however, an adult game. Tell a kid to put back what they worked so hard to catch and you'll lose them at the next Nintendo kiosk.

Recent studies indicate that catch and release methods are harmless only if each fish is released tenderly and with high regard for its delicate condition, not to mention the delicate condition of the fly fisherman. Mortality rates on artificial lures, which fish don't trust to swallow, range as low as 15 percent. Fish gulp hooked live bait and up to 50 percent of those gluttons die. The larger the hook, the larger the mortality of the smaller fish. Release the midsize fish that have a chance for growth into trophies. Contrary to commonly held beliefs, it's okay to take the large female fish as these older matriarchs are getting too crabby anyway. Life expectancy dramatically increases with a stomach-hooked fish if the leader is cut with the hook left in place for stomach acids to eat. More significantly, if you chuck the whole rod and reel into the water, the fish will live a happy life, knowing it outmatched the big boat dummy. You'll also have the purity of soul to afford a new fishing outfit.

✔ *WHEN IS IT APPROPRIATE NOT TO PRACTICE CATCH AND RELEASE?*
- When your brother-in-law is fishing the same hole.
- When your mother-in-law is sitting on the riverbank.
- When you know in your heart of hearts that the trophy wouldn't want to live after being caught on your cheap tackle.

Animal activists are turning their sights under water and arguing that catch and release sport fishing is "having sport at the expense of living creatures." Only the credit card companies have a clue as to the real expense of sport fishing.

Commercial fishermen are under pressure to practice catch and release on anything they don't set out for. If you are a shrimp fisherman working the Gulf of Mexico, you are not supposed to fill the empty corners of your hold with young red snapper, no matter how much leftover blackening seasoning in your kitchen.

FISHING BY SEASON

IN THE SPRING:

✔ *IN NORTHERN WATERS:* Once the ice moves off the lakes and streams and the water warms and absorbs oxygen, fish hormones kick in with the first thoughts of the spawn. When it reaches thirty-five degrees, the surface water sinks and "spring turnover" occurs, confusing the fish as they try to shake off a long winter. Vertigo may occur in the small species.

✔ *IN SOUTHERN, EASTERN, AND WESTERN WATERS:* Baitfishermen are revving their engines for opening day, and fly fishermen continue a midlife crisis into the summer.

IN THE SUMMER:

✔ *IN NORTHERN WATERS:* Those old dog days of summer were named for Sirius, the Dog Star, which rises before the sun in July and August, not for the dogfish you keep hooking into. Every local that doesn't want anything to do with selling bait, beer, or bad advice will apologize for these days of slow fishing, but let Buck tell you, summer can be as good as you like it.

First of all, summer fishing is good for you. It can require little or no activity: just a cane pole, bobber, and a worm. In many parts, it's too damn hot to do anything anyway and fishing becomes one sure way to say you are doing something. You can be abused lying around in the hammock, but if you are fishing, it's sort of work.

Trolling was invented in the early hot days of summer when feminists stopped wives from fanning their fishing hubbies in the hammock. Trolling put you in the boat with a breeze to keep the mosquitoes and black flies at bay. During the first days of trolling, young, impressionable fish thought the fast-moving lures were great fun—at least once.

Warm water slows fish metabolism and, while they may want to eat more, they have a harder time digesting. Some fish just become too lazy to approach a lure so an angler must get his offerings closer to the prey. Locals will say the hot water makes the fish meat soft and are willing to take any large soft walleyes off your hands.

Bass go deep and into vegetation. Trout do most anything precious. Walleyes avoid the midday brightness. Pikes hide in weeds waiting for something to irritate them. Crappies school in the shade, near brush piles or on the long side of ridges or hidden channels.

✔ *IN SOUTHERN WATERS:* It's even hotter. Slow down even more. Drink more beer. Learn and play the banjo.

✔ *IN EASTERN WATERS:* Fish for blues with chum. Good chum is not an acceptable substitute for fish stew, unless you have salt and pepper and your wife's family is coming over.

✔ *IN WESTERN WATERS:* Guide rates escalate along the Front Range. In the Pacific Northwest, anglers wonder what that round, yellow thing in the sky is.

IN THE FALL:

✔ *IN NORTHERN WATERS:* The water begins cooling and a few of the dumber fish like crappies will mistakenly think of spawning when it hits their preferred temperature. The water will continue to cool, however, and the urge is repressed until spring. As the water cools, fish metabolism slows, too. Many fish are larger now, having eaten fishermen's litter all summer. When surface water cools further, it becomes heavier and the fall turnover occurs. For fish experiencing their first turnover, this water inversion can turn the fish upside down, and then you'll have to run your lures below the fish.

✔ *IN SOUTHERN WATERS:* The fishing is easy and the guides in the Florida Keys have the nerve to call their jobs work. Tell your boss to shove it.

✔ *IN EASTERN AND WESTERN COASTAL WATERS:* Migrating and spawning fish provide all the major action.

Fly fishermen call this season autumn.

IN THE WINTER:

✔ *IN NORTHERN WATERS:* The best place to fish is in warmer southern waters. If broke, lake fishermen are resigned to fish familiar waters, only this time they must break through a hard icy crust. The chronology is something like this:

- *SEPTEMBER:* Spend month inspecting ice-fishing house.
- *DECEMBER:* Have brother-in-law test-walk the ice. Four inches of ice is safe enough for your side of the family to walk on, six to seven inches is safe to drive snowmobiles across, and 12 inches minimum is needed to hold up a car or truck. If your brother-in-law falls in, have him climb out on the ice and roll away from the broken edge. Warm him quickly but do not let him crawl inside your snowmobile suit, not matter how cold he says he is.

BUCK'S BONUS TIP: One inch of slushy ice should be thick enough to support your mother-in-law.

- *JANUARY:* Drive wife's car on ice. If safe, pull fish house onto lake.
- *FEBRUARY:* Leave fish house only in case of emergency.
- *LATE MARCH:* Test for slush outside fish house.
- *APRIL:* If fish house is too old or doesn't produce the way it used to, volunteer its unoccupied use to the local chamber of commerce for a fundraising lottery on when it will sink.

    If you are first-generation Scandinavian, you'll set an example of fortitude to those girly-men using heated ice-fishing houses by sitting directly on the ice with only few essentials:

- Ice chisel (or axe spud or auger)
- Skimmer (big spoon with drain holes to keep hole clear)
- Chair (to keep your hemorrhoids from going into cold storage)
- Insulated nut sack (see above)
- Tip-up (to suspend live bait through ice)
- Depth finder with built-in Loran C navigational device
- Hand rod rigged with a bobber, four- to six-pound line, and a #4 to #10 hook

More fish are caught per capita by ice fishermen than by summer enthusiasts. Bass fishermen cut extra-large holes in the frozen lakes for their mosquito boats. To get yourself set up, find where others are fishing and drill a hole nearby. The hole size should be tailored to the species fished. Some states set limits on how big a hole you can drill, dependent on how big a fish they want you to catch. Don't have to ask the quiet lumps on the ice if the fish are biting. The Swedes cherish their quieter moments. If nobody is around, look for an open hole in the ice with equipment left behind. Call 911 once you've had a chance to borrow some of the remaining gear.

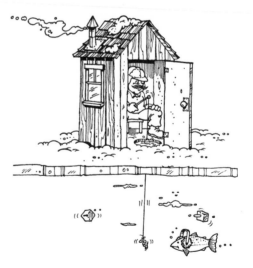

Scoop the ice out of the hole and drop a baited hook in water, close to the bottom. Watch bobber for hours. Blow into hands once an hour and beat sides with arms. Don't stomp on ice—the noise will scare fish and may wake nearby Norwegians. And chestnuts are the only nuts that should be roasted over an open fire.

If snowmobiles buzz you as they try to run down snowshoe rabbits, chop out a few extra holes and leave the blocks of ice covered with snow on their favorite path. Snowmobilers love to plow through fresh powder piles with their helmets on tight, and the sudden stoppage provided by your ice speed bump will shake snoots full of cheap schnapps.

 BUCK'S BONUS TIP: To repel an annoying, crowding ice-fisherman, unwrap and drop a large Baby Ruth candy bar and a few sheets of smudged toilet paper in his ice-hole.

Try to make friends with someone who has a ice house yet too busy to use it. If buying your new friend a cup of coffee isn't enough for an unlimited pass, build your own house, using as little as a refrigerator packing box. Once built, you can either angle, or in a few states, spear fish. The house must be dark for successful spearing. Some spear chuckers throw a handful of sliced potatoes to the bottom so fish passing the hole can be seen more easily. A wood fish decoy is dangled with one hand while the other is filled with a three- to five-tined spear, with tips resting in the water so as not to startle the big fish noses edging into the hole.

Once you've decided to go indoors, your ice house acts like a sound chamber announcing visitors arriving by car. It's difficult to see the game warden with the windows covered, so in many states you are allowed to lock your door from the inside to keep the required concentration. When you buy a "dark" house license, a password is assigned, and the warden must say this password before you are required to open the door. What with all the white-collar crime in the Midwest, this safety precaution is credited with saving lives, not to mention a few reputations.

If you've been real good, the fish gods will completely freeze out a lake with thick ice and deep snow and officials from the Department of Natural Resources will punch emergency oxygen holes through the ice to aerate the waters. The holes are soon stuffed with fish gasping for air and easy for the taking. Gifts such as these are balanced by the new bans on antifreeze to keep fishing holes open. Open-water fanatics must be content to fish the hot water discharges of northern power plants.

✔ *IN SOUTHERN WATERS:* If you live in a warm southern climate, move over. Buck'll be there in a minute, just before dinner. Yes, Buck loves catfish. Your wife won't mind. Believe me, she won't mind.

✔ IN EASTERN WATERS: In the Florida Keys, all the boys are sucking down cold beer, wolfing down plates of fresh boiled shrimp, and finishing off with Key lime pie. In between burps, a little fishing in the flats may happen.

✔ IN WESTERN WATERS: Along the Pacific Northwest, hardy fishermen are out chasing blackmouth, a resident salmon that is smaller than they like. Steel headers are moving slowly and painfully through the many stages of frostbite.

FORECASTS

Fishermen share with hunters a need to predict success, estimates that reach beyond the accuracy of the bumpkin on the porch who nods off with "Ya shoulda been here last week!"

Anthropologists have been fishing for any secrets, patterns, or cycles of subsistence fishermen. Different tribes, including the Maori of New Zealand and bachelor farmers of northern Minnesota, have been interviewed but with little success. One correlation that is commonly accepted is the position of the moon and the best times to catch fish. This system claims that more fish are caught plus or minus two hours of the moon being directly overhead on the days around the new moon phase. Next best time is plus or minus one and a half hours of being straight overhead near the dates of the full moon. The best fishing hours during the moon's first and third quarters are not so good. If all this makes sense, please thank the publisher.

Another forecasting system is the solar/lunar columns found in the front of fishing magazines. These forecasts are described by day and date and should not be shown to anyone dependent on your fishing success, wives in particular. The only dates omitted are the national and personal holidays. The former works best for civil service employees who can stretch three-day holidays into a lifetime of mixed service. For your beloved, it can be predicted that no matter how successful you are on your wedding anniversary it won't make any difference.

Another way to forecast fishing is to predict the tides. Tide, for all you fly-over-country occupants, is the vertical rise and fall of water, not laundry soap. There are generally two high tides and two low tides every day of the last day of your life. Given variations in each tide and since the moon is the stronger source of gravity, tides follow a lunar day (which is fifty minutes longer than a solar day), making tomorrow's tides fifty minutes (or sixteen hectares in Canada) later than today's. Today is yesterday's tomorrow.

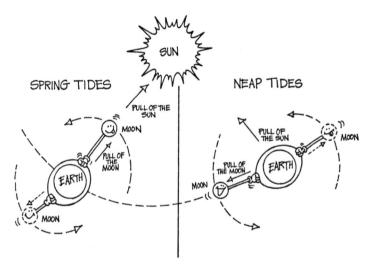

If the sun and the moon are in alignment, as in a new or full moon, spring tides will occur with higher highs and lower lows and strong currents. Neap tides occur at quarter moons with the sun at right angles in the house of Aquarium. Neap tides are the reverse of spring tides. Other influences on tide are winds and barometric pressure; with an onshore wind and dropping barometric pressure, the tides will be higher. Again, the reverse applies. It is also during this time that the PMS tables occur and the higher percentage of water in a woman's body follows the ocean movements. During spring tables, women will leave the home to look for a better paying job, spread gossip about an associate to get ahead, and ask you to take out the garbage more often. The water in their bodies is moving so much during this time that larger women may need restraints.

If you are fishing tidal lakes with a storm moving in and the barometer dropping, good fishing can be expected, but let your brother-in-law carry the steel fishing rod. Fishing in the rain can go either way. It depends more on how wet you want to get. The fish are wet enough. Cloudy days reduce light penetration into the water, making fish feel safer—that's why they are fish and not U-boat commanders. The worst forecast is cold, clear weather following a storm. Fish would rather join you in front of the TV while you watch the bowl games.

If all this empirical information doesn't make you a believer, rely on the more popular grouping of superstitions that deal with weather:

- ✔ Red lips at night, clear skin in the morning
- ✔ Wind from the north, stay in port
- ✔ Wind from the east, fishing's least
- ✔ Winds from the south, fish open their mouth
- ✔ Wind from the west, fishing's best
- ✔ Wind from the bow, your brother-in-law's back

HOW TO BOAT OR BEACH A FISH

After bringing the fish to its almost final end, you have to decide whether to listen to the nattering nabobs about catch and release or just keep the fish, like the good book tells you.

HOW TO BOAT A FISH: Gaffs are stage hooks with sharper points and are indications to a fish that you want their shiny hide hanging on the family room wall. Hook the fish in the jaw and flip aboard. If it's a large, long fish, reach across and over with two gaffs, spaced evenly along the length and roll into the boat.

The most popular method of boating a smaller fish is to use your bare hands. Put your thumb on its lower lip and force its jaw back as you lift the fish out of the water. Research on the lower jaws of bass shows that the excessive strain can damage joints, causing names for released fish, like Old Slackjaw, to be coined. Don't try this technique on the larger billfish without a good pair of gloves.

If you decide against all advice to use a gun and just blast a hole in that five-hundred-pound halibut that refuses to come to Papa, remember that bullets can skip on water. Shoot true. And don't shoot the monster one more time for good measure once it's on the boat unless it's not your boat. Since fish don't heal well from gunshot wounds, this practice is not often used in catch and release.

HOW TO BEACH A FISH: If you don't have any line left or don't want to use any line at all, a properly hooked fish will beach easily if you run directly and swiftly away from the line of retrieve, pulling the fish ashore. Stop running when you've reached the porch, if not before. If you drag the fish for a short distance on the shore, the effort will shorten your scaling time.

If you are on a boat, you can do the same thing by holding the rod out toward shore and running the craft as close to camp as possible. If it's a big fish, drive the boat right onto the trailer and have a friend pull the entire rig and tackle out of the water.

If you can't boat the fish, tow it by tying a tail rope to the stern cleat with its mouth roped shut. Understand that's how Hemingway's Old Man lost his fish but then again, that book is fiction. If it's a real big fish, tow it along side so skunked fishermen (losers!) can't harpoon it. Don't run up the fishing flag until your brother-in-law on shore can see it.

HOW TO SELECT A GUIDED TRIP

How much time do you have? If you just have a weekend, fish local waters with a topnotch guide. If you have a week, you can count on at least five good days of fishing most anywhere in the world. If you have more than a week, you are part of the world's larger problems and should be ashamed.

What kind of fish do you want to catch? Do you want a trophy fish and/or a trophy stringer? Do you want an exotic fish that your neighbor will never catch? If you had your druthers and/or money, would you rather go to Iceland or Alaska for salmon? Realize that you can't catch bonefish in northern Wisconsin, regardless of what the local chamber of commerce says. Boneheads are a different story, however.

What kind of fishing do you want to do? Do you want to fish like the natives, fly-fish, bait-fish, fish with heavy explosives? Do you want to sleep in a tent, in a fixed camp, or have a bush pilot pick you off the dock for truly inaccessible (to your estranged family) fishing? Do not read any further until you've answered these questions.

HOW TO SELECT THE GUIDE: The four key questions to ask a potential guide are: How are they biting? Do you like to fish? Do I have to bring my own worms? What's the wife's name?

It helps to know how long the guide has been fishing and how successful he has been. Watch out for artificially seasoned young guides, you know the type, local dipsticks that imitate the worn trappings and cranky nature of retired guides to lend credence to being the old man of the river, lake, deep briny, and the higher rate schedule. If the young guide is a fly fisherman, he will compete with his peers as to who's more curmudgeonly, with the crankiest winning a year's subscription to *The New Yorker*, a dozen waterproof business cards, and a good stool softener.

Another good indicator of the guide's ability is the state of his equipment. If you are planning to fish flat river water and the boy shows up in a new Mackenzie boat, the rates will skyrocket due to the heavy mortgages involved.

If you decide to tip the guide before you start the trip, the gesture establishes your good faith and the guide may let his wife sleep with you if the fishing is poor.

HOW TO BOOK A GUIDED TRIP: After sucking down half a rack of beer while watching a fishing program on cable TV, it's not hard to drift off in your easy chair dreaming of fishing for humongous fish in the icy waters of the northern frontier.

Make this a reality by attending a sportsman's show for the latest exaggerations. Don't bother talking to the young guides because they are busy dropping mickeys in the soft drinks of the big-breasted women working the ticket gates, and recruiting for cook and hook jobs back at the lodge.

A FEW TIPS ON FINDING THE BEST FISHING LODGE: Call the lodge at 5:00 A.M. and ask how the weather is and call at 10 P.M. to find out how they did. Call collect. At midnight, with a handkerchief over the mouthpiece, call the local warden to ask how the lodge did. Compare the stories.

Always ask for the owner's wife. She's less likely to stretch the truth and, after listening to fish stories all season, appreciates hearing from a friendly outsider, especially one with your aberrant sexual habits.

Shop around for the best price. Start by asking for their most deluxe packages and work down to the "insider," or resident package that includes the bait. Warn them that your fishing partner is the ACLU attorney who busted the Hawaiians for selling cheaper food to the natives. Never ask what currencies they take. Canadian lodges want hard U.S. currency and will often refuse their own North American equivalent of rubles.

In a very tough world where you just can't believe anybody, requirements for deposits are just a formality. When they ask for a fixed percentage up front, plead for as much time as you need to sneak the money out of the little woman's checking account and write a check, postdated with your arrival date. By the time you pass a number of checks back and forth, you'll either be there or not.

Big game fishing is expensive. For example, salmon trips to Iceland run over one thousand dollars a day plus a required listening to early Björk albums. Norway is even more expensive but the rates include multiple layer wrapping for any lutefisk purchased while there.

FISHING FOR THE EXOTICS

✔ *DISTRESSED FISH:* For fish lounging in the hot waters surrounding an atomic power plant, night fishing is very effective. It isn't necessary to read the waters, just push the Geiger counter button on your depth finder.

✔ *DYING FISH:* As it expires due to low water conditions or a million other reasons, a fish will lie on its side and you must cast sideways to hit its mouth. In this condition, a fish will not be very aggressive and may not strike normally. Pinpoint accuracy is the key.

✔ *FLYING FISH:* Seem to jump high out of the water and fly on large pectoral fins and are sent by the salmon gods to distract you. An all-around sportsman will take the opportunity to practice his wing-shot skills. It's not necessary to lead by much.

✔ *HYBRID FISH:* The general rule is to fish for the dominant characteristics. For example, if the dominant breed is a muskie, use techniques and tackle to catch that species as the recessive other half will go along for the ride.

✔ *NONRESIDENT FISH:* In the final analysis, these fish really belong to you, the local taxpayer. While the letter of the law may not support you, the spirit might as you flash an imitation badge to review the catch, confiscating as needed for marine research.

✔ *THEME PARK/RESORT FISH:* While the resort hotel security thugs are taping the action in the honeymoon suites, drag a treble hook through the koi ponds for the catch of the day.

✔ *WALKING FISH:* A catfish variety imported from Asia for aquariums that escaped from southern Florida fish farms into coastal waters. Walking fish have no known predators but fish biologists are hoping to get the Asian dogfish walking real soon.

FISHING AROUND THE WORLD

In the Philippines, fishermen use cyanide illegally to stun fish for the aquarium trade. Large quantities of this chemical marked "To Be Used Only during a General Election" were found in the Marcos palace.

Northwest Indians used to fish for lingcod with the "hee hees." The natives would use a long spear and a lure that looked like a shuttlecock. The lure was pushed to the bottom, and as the buoyant shuttlecock spun to the surface, a fish would follow it in hot pursuit. The fish would be speared as it came into view. The tribe that used this technique exclusively is now extinct. The French urgently need more fish flesh to use up the remaining hollandaise sauce purchased from the Netherlands under the Marshall Plan.

Fishing in the lost empire of Great Britain is too confusing—too many fishermen with too many opinions and no respect for the new generation of buzz baits.

In Canada, residents are no longer able to shoot fish given their restrictive gun control laws. Americans, in most areas, however can take as many fish as they like just as long as they close the gate before crossing the border back into the United States

The islands of Japan have few sport fishing opportunities, and most would-be fishermen have turned their genetic fanaticism towards golf, which is similar to fly-fishing in its reverence for the object of play, extravagance in equipment, silly-looking clothing, and allegiance to grand masters. The few remaining angling opportunities occur in the ponds of Shinto shrines. Their obese goldfish are raised for foreign visitors and easily snagged during the tea ceremony.

FISHING BOAT BEHAVIOR

✔ *HOW TO MAN THE BOAT:* There are two positions in smaller fishing boats, front or back. If you are in a rowboat, those in the bow (front) must handle the anchor, tie up at the dock, and get splashed on a windy day. Those in the stern (back) must either row or handle the motor. If you are up front in a canoe, your job is to help paddle but, more important, to steer, which can mean not pulling your full load. The guy with the big shoulders in the back is the power paddle. Who gets the comfortable chair in a bass boat? The owner.

✔ *HOW TO BOARD THE BOAT:* To use a boat, you have to get into it. (If I'm going too slowly, it's because this information is real important.) If you are able to transport yourself to exactly one spot in the middle of the boat with perfect balance, go ahead and jump. Many fishermen enter the boat carefully by hanging onto something hard like a mother-in-law's head and stepping into the middle of the boat from the dock. Once aboard, help others, shifting your weight as a counterbalance for the in-law dead weight now arriving. Then load equipment and whistle for the fat dog that will tip the boat.

✔ *HOW TO AVOID GETTING WET ON THE BOAT:* Even Buck can't help you here.

✔ *HOW TO GO TO THE TOILET ON THE BOAT:* Boat bottles for both men and women to go number one are available wherever fine toiletries are sold. They are shaped like gourds and the women's version has a special baffle top, designed to cover the little fluffers denied while toileting. If only men are in the boat, just stand up, spit, and relieve yourself over the side. Aim downwind and for practice, at your partner's bobber.

 BUCK'S BONUS TIP: In the adrenaline rush of fishing, women's sexual drives are at their highest peak, so don't show her your "package" unless you want to miss the morning feeding.

There are no provisions to go number two (or Big Job) on a small boat. You'll have to pull anchor and head for shore. Be considerate of others. Cover with dirt. Or bag and declare your dump at the border crossing.

✔ *HOW TO DRINK AND DRIVE FAST ON THE BOAT:* Spoilsports are claiming that over fifty thousand boating accidents a year are caused by drinking. Then again, water-skiers have always had drinking problems. Some states like Wyoming treat drunk boaters like drunk drivers, and the sheriff assigned to patrol the lakes of the Equality State says he'll get right on it as soon as he can get that darn-fangled Japanese motor started. Other states are looking at legislation that would make the mere possession of alcohol on a boat a crime, with the only exception being peach-flavored wine coolers in Southern California, but then what peach flavoring does to alcohol is a crime too.

✔ *HOW TO DOCK THE BOAT:* Approach the dock with the wind either at your back or in your face. Avoid any bubbles near scuba diving signs. Approach the dock slowly unless you want to thrill the kids playing on the beach. Have a mate throw a line to dockhand. Tie stern on opposite cleat and then tie bow. Take motor out of gear before the line snaps.

✔ *HOW TO NAME THE BOAT:* Much like naming a child, your boat must be properly identified. If you are like every other boat buyer, name it after the owner—Busted.

✔ *PARTY BOATS (PUKERS):* For many part-time fishermen, charter party boats are the easiest way to catch fish. You can go out for a half a day or a whole day; while both may seem the same, the prices are different. Make reservations, show up with your dirty shirt and a five-dollar bill, and drink your buddies' beer all day long. Boat boys bait your hook and remove your catch. Just jam the butt end in a rod holder and go below to cheat on cards with the captain.

If you want a good position, show up early. When the others arrive, demand to board first, mumbling something about being first mate. Fishing from the bouncing bow not only give you more line action but makes you sort of captain. Enjoy the feeling and bark a few orders to your mates down the stern.

Fishing from the more stable stern keeps your bait from bouncing up off the bottom, but the diesel fumes will attract the pickled eggs, dried beef sticks, and curdled beer floating just below the epiglottis.

Which leads to the most important lesson on party boats: where to throw up? If you feel the urge for a "personal protein spill," select a proper perch. If you are hanging off the bow and the captain is heading into the wind, you'll have to work a little harder, like a good tenor clearing his throat before a concert. Cup your mouth and yell through your hands like you are calling fathom markers. You may mess the side of the boat, but the surf will take care of that.

Older boats have toilets so small that you can't properly hug the porcelain, so you may have to do this standing up. The small porthole should be opened and used if you can't get it all in the bowl. The main thing is not to get any on your new fishing outfit and to look like all you did was go poop (#2). Stay in the john long enough for your eyes to clear and the spittle to dry in your mustache.

Have you noticed that you never see the captain or deckhands throw up? They will after seeing your gratuity. Or using the boat toilet after you.

Before you return to the pier, boat boys will be cleaning fish, and when the others are puking, it's time to cut a deal for the choice fillets before they are democratically divided and dumped into individual bags. If you are a non-resident, tell the boy your wallet is in the car and you'll take care of him as soon as you dock. He'll never recognize you again—you are just another sunburned, drunk, low roller the captain described as he hid his rain checks.

PIER PRESSURE

In Minnesota, piers are called docks. The docks are wheeled into the water after the ice is off the lake. In addition to fishing platforms, docks are launchpads for water-skiers, tie-ups for boats and beer, and a roof over a quiet place to play marine doctor with the girl next door.

Most importantly docks are where you can learn to fish from. You don't need a boat. If you sit close enough to shore, you can keep your feet cool in the water and all your paraphernalia can be spread around you. If you snag a large fish, run up the dock and beach the monster. If you get tired or hungry or thirsty, you are just footsteps away from the cabin where your folks are playing cards with Jack Daniels and Jim Beam.

A pier is a large dock with substantial pilings and railings that the beach master leaves in the water year round. If the pier is set in tidal water, sometimes the water is there, sometimes it's not. The tide schedule is timed to coincide with the departure and arrival schedule of nonresident fishermen. The locals will also tell you that the fish leave when the water leaves, but under close scrutiny, this phenomenon is only partly true. The fish that decide to remain are kept in the small buckets the Vietnamese at the end of the dock are hiding. The larger buckets hold their elders, who appreciate their children's respect.

Fish from a pier on a strongly rising or falling tide, weakly falling or rising tides, and at peak tides or whenever it's best for you and your new "camp" wife. A drop line with live bait is best on the bottom with a slack tide. If you have casting gear, fish up current and retrieve back toward the pilings, criss-crossing the supports as much as possible. If down current, walk the lure up or down the length of the pier, saying "excuse me" as needed. When you hook a fish off a pier, the fish is a long way down so the better part of your retrieve is out of the water. Move your rod frequently to simulate a little action. This maneuver will also skin, scale, or calm any fish that you bring up.

Fly-fishing off a pier is certain to raise a few hackles.

OTHER WAYS OF DOING BUSINESS

If you don't want to feed the hand that equips the rush to gear, here are some other traditional ways to fish.

✔ *BOW FISHING:* Incorporating the skills of stealth, strength, and surprise and for those obvious reasons, bow fishing is limited by law to rough fish. Carp are not pleased to be singled out this way.

BUCK'S BONUS TIP: California law requires the use of rubber-tipped arrows while bowfishing for surfers.

✔ *CATCH BY HAND:* States like Mississippi allow a short grappling season, when fish can be caught either by hand or with grappling tongs. Experienced hands can fill a stringer. You can identify a good grappler by his extra-long arms and the strained look on his face.

✔ *EMERGENCY LINES AND HOOKS:* Line has been made of most everything: thin strips of bark, horsehair, seaweed, and in an emergency, braided pubic hair. Native hooks were made of wood (shank) and bone or shells (bend and point). An effective lure was a pencil-size hardwood stick sharpened on both ends and inserted lengthwise into a minnow. Once set hard by the angler, the points would stick into the swallower's throat and the surprised fish could be easily retrieved.

✔ *EXPLOSIVES:* In a few of the marine life conservation districts of Hawaii, you can fish with bang sticks, powerheads, and even carbon dioxide injections—all the more reason to vacation there. Have the bellman at the Marriott store your gear.

On the heels of free postage, a perk the Armed Forces recruiters don't mention is the ability to fish with grenades while in a war zone. Buck used to time the grenades to explode just below the water surface in Vietnam and the stunned fish would float to shore, along with some really irritated U.S. Navy SEAL teams working the area.

✔ *HERDING FISH:* A herd of natives would circle a school of fish and chase them into either an enclosure or a natural pool where they could be speared. Any attempt to move fish in the Great Lakes is limited to fishermen who can hold their breath for more than ten minutes.

✔ *NUMB WITH PLANTS:* Only locals knew which plants emitted chemicals that would numb not only the fish but the fishermen. There is evidence that certain hallucinogenic fungi were used in traditional ceremonies. However, these practices were curtailed once the natives discovered how good those mushroom buttons went with buffalo steaks.

✔ *TRAPS (OR WEIRS):* Commonly used by natives and survivalists. Sticks and stones drive the fish into a brushy entrance and an escape-proof enclosure. This technique is most commonly used now by bass tournament fishermen.

HAZARDS OF FISHING

✔ *ANGLER'S ELBOW:* The same inflammation that affects tennis tendons is showing up in hard-core anglers, particularly with fly fishermen spending too much time casting upwind. The tendonitis can be cured by stopping fishing and lying on your couch all weekend, shooting up with cortisone and finishing with a nice port wine and fresh brie.

✔ *HOOKS IN SKINS:* A well-placed hook is a badge of courage. If you must, tear it out and the scar will distinguish you among your German dueling friends.

✔ *LEAD POISONING:* Frequent handling of lead jigs by tournament fishermen can further reduce the angler's intelligence, memory, coordination, and concentration. Ditto using your own dentures on split-shot.

✔ *MOSQUITOES:* Welcome that buxom lady ringing your chimes and ask for Skin So Soft, remarking how it keeps your skin so luxuriously moist. If you buy a case of this good-smelling repellant or volunteer to be a distributor, she is trained to rub a sample on your most sensitive parts.

As could be predicted, only pregnant female mosquitoes bite humans. A manufacturer has introduced a sound machine that imitates the sound of the male mosquito that is avoided since it was he that made her that way in the first place. Research continues.

✔ *SAND FLEAS, BODY LICE, HANGOVERS:* Don't bring any home.

✔ *SEXUALLY TRANSMITTED DISEASES OF MYSTERIOUS ORIGIN:* The frequency of these maladies is in direct proportion to the miles away from home. If you promise to take the family physician on the next fishing trip, he'll load you up with a preventative dose of wide-spectrum antibiotic to cover most social occasions.

✔ *STRUCK BY LIGHTNING:* If you are caught in an electric thunderstorm, give your brother-in-law your antique steel fishing rod and lay down in the bottom of the boat. If you are struck by lightning, relax. You can replace the soles of your shoes later.

A FEW SELECT WHITE LIES

FOR YOUR BROTHER-IN-LAW

You can see the fish better from the bow.
That lure worked before.
I'll row next.
I'll pay you back later.
You really are a good guy!

FOR THE WARDEN

We're just saving the smaller fish so we don't catch
them over and over again. We'll let them go later.
It's in my other wallet, other pants, in the car, truck, at
home, in the garage. My dog ate it. My wife washed it.
My kids pawned it.
Sure, I know what a slot limit is.
I don't know how that got there.
This is how we do it back home.

FOR YOUR WIFE

That is not lipstick.
I sure like your brother.

CONVERSATION STARTERS IN THE TAVERN

We nonresidents pay your wages.
Husband here with you, honey?
Do you call that a full shot?
Yeah, says who?

FISHING
BY
FISH

FISHING FOR FRESHWATER FISH

Freshwater is limited to smaller quantities, but as most fly fishermen know, even small things can have value. Freshwater fisherman can be found avoiding lawn work on these waters.

✔ *MANMADE RESERVOIRS OR PONDS:* Come in all sizes and over 27 million anglers waste 350 million days on these more predictable waters.

✔ *NATURAL LAKES AND PONDS:* Approximately 15 million anglers drink beer over 193 million days a year when fishing these waters, and if the aluminum cans were placed end to end, NASA astronauts could walk to Uranus. Given how their airships work, this might not be a bad idea.

✔ *NATURAL RIVERS AND STREAMS:* More than 17 million anglers lie to each other on these banks for what seems like 250 million days. Fly-fishing novices waiting for genuine camaraderie and bonhomie from the senior purists will have to wait for the 251 millionth day.

✔ *SPRINGWATER:* Fish do not normally swim in the special spring waters necessary to making good beer, but one species of suckers is attracted to the naturally bubbly waters just uphill from Paris, near the town of Perrier.

AN OVERSTUFFED TACKLE BOX OF FRESHWATER TIPS

✔ *CARP:* With their small mouths, use a small #4 hook on six- to eight-pound test line and baited with a dough ball made from bread mixed with cornmeal and milk. The Asian silver or jumping carp are best swatted with a badminton or tennis racket. Carp are omnivorous, and while they may not eat all their vegetables, try marinating broccoli in a fish sauce and you'll have found a way to use this awful green vegetable.

✔ *CATFISH:* Most dramatically caught by a technique called grappling. Wade in the deep catfish water and stick your hand in the deep, dark holes under the banks that hide the big cats. The monster will think it is a dead rat and, with luck, will suck your hand into its whiskered hole. Once inside, grab its gill plate, and with feet propped up against the riverbank, pull the behemoth out of its cave. Once both of you are able to discuss who goes up the bank first, have your fishing partner start the winch motor.

   In a few communities, it's legal to call catfish on the telephone. For electro fishing to work properly, drop two wires into the catfish holes and hand crank the old-fashioned generator to see if anyone is home. Alternative long-distance carriers are offering cheaper rates to fishermen who fish from long distances.

   • *FLATHEADS:* Much like those who fish for them, the largest catfish are recognized by the flat surface between the eyes and a lower jaw that is longer than the upper. Use big gear with big sucker minnows over shallow flats or structures and cover. At night, avoid motors and lights. Another almost approved technique is a trotline.

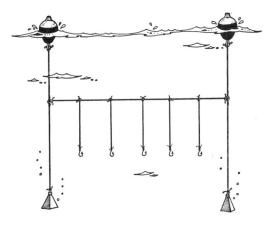

Catfish senses aren't sensitive, so most anything that is turning sour can be used as bait. Some fishermen use beef brains soaked in fish oil, others come over and take most anything in Buck's refrigerator.

✔ *CRAPPIES:* Crappies are a schooling fish so if you catch one, there will be more. Handle the first one carefully, put a hook through its tail and let it swim back to the school where it will tell its friends that you are practicing catch and release.

✔ *MUSKELLUNGE:* Use big bait with rods bigger than you, big reels with drag ratios of a power winch, and miles of heavy Dacron line. Muskies are sight feeders and can be stimulated into action by trolling spinners, buck tails, deep-running crank baits, large spoons, and small dogs. Because of their sharp teeth, use wire leaders and cast far from the boat. Really big muskies will think your outboard motor prop is a big spinner prop so keep a harpoon handy. If you see a muskie following your lure up to the boat, figure eight the final retrieve and keep any loose skin from hanging over the side of the boat. For a ringside seat on the marine channel of Wrestlemania, hand the rod to the smallest person in the boat.

✔ *PERCH:* Just pretend you are fishing for crappies.

✔ *PIKE:* The speedsters and bullies of the weed beds. While they won't hit right before or during spawn, right after the hospital closes, they will hit, not just bite, anything—up to a fish half their size. Northerns are a fisherman's dream—striking until they get it right. Fish with live shiners on a bobber, troll with flashy spoons or deep-diving plugs, or cast "action" plugs along weed beds. They aren't big night feeders but when they stop, their big brother, the muskie, starts.

✔ *STRIPERS:* When they are feeding on a school of shad, throw different lures at them until one works. Use larger, tougher gear. When they are running along the coast.

✔ *STURGEON:* Regulations on this fish change so quickly that you'll have to call the warden at home. If he responds a bit rudely to your friendly requests, regardless of the hour, tell him you are a taxpayer and that he works for you. Use your brother-in-law's name.

✔ *SUCKERS:* Can be hooked off or near the bottom but the most fun is to spear them during spawning runs. Buck speared his first sucker near a stone arch in central Minnesota. Champion spearers can put more than one sucker on each spearhead, better yet one per tine, and flipping them to shore or at a buddy downstream.

✔ *TILAPIA:* This farmed fish is listed in the regs as "Catch of the Day" and, in most habitats, hidden in a light batter.

✔ *TROUT:* The publishing community embraces the literary aspirations and conspiracies of the trout fisherman, especially those who fly-fish. The general technique can be reduced to carefully approaching the water low to the ground and hitting them when they are feeding on insects in the early evening hatch. Trout are very predictable in their biting habits, regardless of the smoke screens and veils hung by the majordomos, and no matter what a fly fisherman says, a trout brain is the same size as a bass brain. In streams, fish those areas where the flow gathers food, like downstream of bait casters eating their Spam sandwiches. If all else fails, Mepps spinners work great unless the river has been electro-shocked recently by the local fish and game department.

- *CUTTHROAT:* Several strains, like the Colorado River cutthroat, are strictly regulated so it's important to read all the regulations first. If you accidentally take one, wrap the fish carefully in an oilcloth and send to the state fish and game research department, including a return address so they can send you a thank-you note and two cassettes of John Denver's Greatest Hits.
- *LAKE TROUT:* Lake trout feed almost always during the day and in shallow water, so use a fishing spoon or still-fish with live bait. In deeper water, troll spoons and Rapalas using downriggers. In Canada, make sure to fish upwind of any U.S. power plant.
- *RAINBOW TROUT:* Papa H. once called fishing for big western rainbows "a wild and frazzling sport." Or maybe he was describing sex on the Pilar. Rainbows prefer to be caught in the late afternoon and in the cooler waters of spring and early summer. If you follow the instructions they'll give up on dry and wet flies, nymphs, streamers, spoons, bait, marshmallows, nose boogers, or most anything on special at your local Fart Mart.

✔ *STEELHEAD:* In the Pacific Northwest, the sea-run rainbows can be caught whenever it is snowing, sleeting, or fifty degrees below zero without wind chill. Steelheaders are the hardiest and the fastest freshwater fish. Drift fishing will most likely do it. But there probably aren't any fish in your river today. Sorry.

✔ *WALLEYES:* Walleyes like overcast skies and darker waters due to their sensitive eyes. If you must fish clear water, fish early and late in the day in the spring and fall when the sun is in the house of Aquarium. Or when your head is in Uranus.

You can catch all the above and more with a rod that's as tall as you are, one reel of your choice, five dollars of line, a handful of terminal tackle, and a ten-dollar allowance of minnows, worms, condoms, and lures. Don't let anyone tell you different and certainly don't tell your wife.

FISHING FOR SALTWATER FISH

Statistically, a third of all "salts" venture at least three miles out and the third that don't drown use a boat. Another third fish within three miles of shore but beyond the surf. Almost half of all saltwater sport fishing is done in the surf with a spinning rod a little taller than you are, a ten-pound test line, a two-hook bottom rig baited with blood worms, a half rack of cold beer, and six jumbo condoms. Tidal sounds and bays capture a good number of the fly-fishing boneheads, and for this group, leave the instructions on the condoms. A very small group will fish the tidal rivers and streams, and their drift boats pass shacks with front porches full of towheaded youngsters whose widely spaced, blank stares can't recognize that they bear a remarkably close resemblance to their first cousins. The major difference between fishing the East and West Coasts is tighty whities and boxers. The major difference between the northern and southern coastlines is cultural and to attract a larger reading public, Buck doesn't want to reopen old wounds. In many quarters, Buck is called "The Healer" due to his accomplished bedside manner.

AN OVERSTUFFED TACKLE BOX OF SALTWATER TIPS

✔ *ALBACORE:* A big member of the tuna family that migrates from Japan to Baja, Baja to Canada, and then back to Hawaii before the quota on Japanese tourists is filled. Albacore schools are located by trolling with feathered jigs and cause a fever successfully treated only on a charter boat.

✔ *ANCHOVIES:* Speared by gourmands in the bottom of any good Caesar salad, this small pickled and salted marine species is also found captive wherever "hold the anchovies" is said.

✔ *BILLFISH:* Except for striped marlin that can be spotted and baited, all billfish can be caught by high-speed trolling dead bait. The higher the speed, the deader the bait. The bill to catch this fish is high.

✔ *BLUES:* A major game fish along the eastern shoreline. In the late spring, small blues or "snappers" will attack minnows or flashy metal lures dropped along jetties and cape shoals, whatever cape shoals are. The adult "choppers" come later, and anglers gear up with tall rods, lots of fifteen-pound test line, a rack of longnecks, a bucket of puke from last night's hospitality suite, three condoms, and either big plugs with eagle hooks and live, fresh mullet, or with two beach bunnies in tank tops.

✔ *BONEFISH:* In a neat twist of fish fate, one of the best bonefish killing fields is in Hawaii, off the north shore of Hanalei, where conditions force an angler to cast or bottom-fish with live bait. Fly fishermen are allowed to observe and weep.

✔ *COD:* What party boat captains fill their boat's body bags with. Cod can be found near the bottom, and most anything dead impaled on a hook with bring this popular breaded blue plate special to you.

✔ *DOLPHIN:* Tuna boat captains and crew fish for dolphins with billy clubs and twelve-gauge shotguns. Oops, wrong fish. Dolphin, or more accurately *Coryphaena hippuru*, are prized fighters and are normally caught while trolling surface lures for billfish.

✔ *GROUPER:* A family with over four hundred members. Jeez, you'd think they practice birth control. If you practice catch and release, do the fish world a favor and cut off the male fish's "unit" before returning him to the water.

✔ *HALIBUT:* A deep-water fish. Twelve-ounce sinkers will get you down to the 250-foot level, but you may need more weight to pull these garage doors off the bottom. Cheeks (face, not butt) are the delicacy.

✔ *MACKEREL:* Schooling fish that can be spotted by the oil slicks from feeding frenzies during which they will eat anything. Holy Mackerel is served in the Vatican's employee cafeteria on Friday's only.

✔ *MARLIN:* Like all billfish, marlins are caught by trolling with bait or flashy lures behind expensive boats and turned into fish sausage by the Japanese.

✔ *POLLACK:* As a group, all that's needed to catch a large Pollack is a flashing neon line. If they don't seem to be biting, chum with hard-boiled eggs and beef jerky sticks.

✔ *SALMON:* There are whole schools of salmon fishermen, and most don't belong to clubs, societies, or participate in tournaments. In the Atlantic Northeast, the reverse is generally true. Natives of the Pacific Northwest believe that the season's first salmon caught is the fish god testing the harvest. Described in peyote dream analysis as resembling Judge George Boldt, the fish god, once eaten, returns to the magic kingdom under the sea for another year of dodging Japanese drift netters. Recently, the high Japanese fisheries Minister said the scientific principle tested by drift netting is one of physics: exactly how many salmon a drift net can strangle before it breaks.

Mooching, the term coming from the Pacific Northwest Indian term that translated roughly to "white men coming to borrow more land," is a popular salmon technique. Large groups of moochers can be found at any

Scandinavian family reunion. Mooching rods should be tall with a firm butt and a light head and so rigged are called Swedish fish sticks. Anchovies saved from yesterday's Caesar salad work well as bait.

In certain parts of the country, spawning salmon struggling the last few miles can be snagged with treble hooks. Local experts say, "This isn't really a sport, but excuse me, I think I have one on."

- *ATLANTIC:* Caught with stink bait, halibut lures, hand grenades, and barbless catch and release treble hooks.
- *BOOT SALMON:* The smaller, least noticeable catch. To retrieve a boot salmon, reach deep into your waders and pull out a choice silver for a midday captain's lunch.
- *CHINOOK, OR KING:* Chinook stop feeding once they enter freshwater, so either take them in salt water with bait or irritate them with most anything else up river. Any chinook over fifty pounds is called a tyee, and if you've caught one, it's time to tyee one on.
- *CHUM:* Primarily a commercial fish and called dog salmon by its detractors. The largest of these salmon are called trophy chum salmon by P. Richter, famous professional Alaskan guide, who used to guide

fishermen from the "outside" along the Yukon River until the native children hooted him out of the village.

- *COHO OR SILVER:* Surface feeders that will hit most anything while in school, preferring flashers and dodgers ahead of cut herring.
- *HATCHERY:* Never really certain when the spawn is to begin, so keep your detection gear handy for indication of these fish bumping their thick skulls along the coastline.
- *PINK OR HUMPIES:* The least valuable salmon and best caught out of a #10 can.
- *SOCKEYE OR RED:* Experts say jig-style fishing on a slow retrieve with spinning tackle may work. The kokanee, a landlocked nonmigratory freshwater relative, is starting to attract dry flies.

✔ *SHARK:* Most popularly caught at night by gillnetters and in the day by accidental discharge of a large-bore firearm.

✔ *STRIPERS:* Cast seventy-five to one hundred yards out into the surf, using ten-plus fly rods, open reels, twenty-five-pound line, and live bait. Reel in when breakers roll in, let drop back when the surf recedes. By the way, the young tank tops playing beach blanket bingo behind you aren't interested in your condom collection.

✔ *SWORDFISH:* A troubled resource but if you must, use squid bait on top of five lines that range out from twenty-five to three hundred feet, using eighteen-foot leaders and four-hundred-pound test mono. When you see a tap on the line, go to free spool, count to ten or one thousand (Buck forgets), and set the hook. The doctor will re-attach your arms when you get back to the dock.

✔ *TUNA:* To catch these nomads, follow the warm water—58 to 68 degrees Fahrenheit (200 degrees Centrifugal in Canada). Using 150-pound-class rods and reels and 250-pound mono line with chum and strap yourself tightly into a fighting chair so the ship doctor will have a stationary carcass to sew shoulders back on.

If it seems like you can catch most of the above with just heavy gear trolling dead bait or flashy lures behind expensive boats, surprise, you can. It's a simpler world on salt water and a real man can meet his match at sea. No wonder Papa H didn't write The Old Man and the Trout Stream.

FLY-FI$HING
AS AN
ART FORM
AND
SOCIAL
DYSFUNCTION

FLY-FISHING AS AN ART FORM AND SOCIAL DYSFUNCTION

Buck's fly-fishing buddies have begged to have their vision printed as a separate book, and if not that, to at least occupy the front part of this book. If not that, to at least have their copy double-spaced and bold. If not that, at least hand lettered in fine Old English script. The publisher rejected all these suggestions.

Standard references have been written on almost all species of game fish fished under almost all conditions and with almost all types of tackle. Once trout are finally finished off in the last environmental gridlock, material will be available on fly-fishing for the surviving alligator gar. The publisher and Buck agree that this guidebook has the potential to become a small classic and that fly-fishing bibliophiles will overlook the softcover on account of the publisher says it makes it more accessible to baitfishermen.

RODS

The first fly rods were made from hazel, aspen, hickory, greenheart, ash, and fir. Occasionally, two or three woods were used—hickory for the butt end and greenheart for the top. Then came bamboo, either whole or split and then reglued. Bamboo rods were often impregnated with preservatives to give strength. Fiberglass, both hollow and solid, followed during the 1940s, and the growth of the use of boron and graphite paralleled the increasing technological needs of today's fisherman. Higher modulus graphite in all composite strengths continues to lighten the burden of the midstream muddler and rods of the future will be as ethereal as the art form itself.

For the proper rod, seek the unbiased opinion of a fly rod shop owner or you can select a rod by analyzing your fishing techniques and conditions. Rods with rigid tips whip the line out better, medium tips go medium distances, and limber tips delicately lay line by the fish lying at your feet. The rod butt is always covered by cork and the reel always hangs below the rod, should you forget.

Many manufacturers have fly-fishing starter kits that give the beginner enough "stuff" to see if they want to graduate to more expensive rods with greater line speed and control. The musty, encrusted old-line companies make rods just for sleepovers at a friend's fishing lodge. All fly-fishing rods are sold by length, the recommended line weight, and number of sections. If you can't afford a bamboo rod, buy a graphite rod with "bamboo like" action. If you can't afford a graphite rod, buy a fiberglass rod with "graphite like" action (and fish more downstream). If you can't sneak enough out of the joint checking account to afford a fiberglass rod, forget it. Your wife is calling. You've got to go now.

If you travel any distance to fly-fish, buy a rod that comes in sections. The encased rod can travel with you as carry-on luggage so your fishing trip can't be ruined by the gorillas in the baggage room. When you reassemble the rod, an old custom in the established northeast lodges is to lubricate the ferrules by lightly sticking them up your nose. If the ferrules are real loose, try to catch a booger or two so your rod tip won't fly off during a power haul.

The newer, more sensitive graphite rods are designed for the newer, more sensitive fisherman, and the buyer's guide will dictate a specific numbered line for a specific numbered rod. For example, if you bought a number eight rod, you'd have to fish with a number eight line or else. The older rods were more forgiving or forgetful in that they'd allow one line size larger or smaller without too much trouble. Excusing an opinion from any purist river guide, that is.

Rod and reel systems eliminate angler anxiety and include the rod, reel, specific line, and recommendations on proper apparel. Any system will do well. A number nine will take most of the smaller salt- and freshwater species while you'd best rig at least two of these in tandem for anything larger.

REELS

Fly-fishing reels are designed primarily to store fly line. The fancier ones are designed for a deep line of credit at the fly-line store. Fly line is looped out by hand for casting, and in drag can be used to retrieve large game fish. Fly reels don't have the multiple gear ratios of a spinning reel and are usually one spool revolution to each complete turn of the handle, except in Canada where the French support a more general revolution.

Fly-fishing reels are larger than spinning reels in order to carry the long lengths of "backing" tied to the tapered line that is cast. In saltwater tournament fishing, you may need up to five hundred yards of backing attached to a ninety-foot fly line, not to mention the financial backing necessary to keep your tuna tower afloat. Freshwater fishing requires a lot less backing, but the larger reels afford trout fishermen the self-esteem necessary to the smaller creels.

Fly-fishing reels are objects of beauty, often machined from solid, anodized aluminum blocks and hand polished to a high sheen before being lovingly placed in a custom leather bag. The new reels incorporate sophisticated drag systems, left- or right-hand retrieve models, interchangeable spools, and the options of direct drive or anti-reverse.

Many fly-fishing reels are sold with separate price tags for the reel and spoon, and manufacturers warn against the unauthorized use of less expensive "foreign" parts. Reminder: fly-fishing reels are to hang below the rod, left or right according to the gentleman's custom.

LINE

Fly-fishing line provides the weight necessary to carry the fly to the fish. Its second purpose is to load the rod, causing a fleeting moment of man and rod ecstasy. The third and less discussed reason for its being is to engage the fish in a flesh-ripping struggle for existential supremacy.

The first fly line was braided horsehair and was used until all the horse butts were picked clean. The oriental imports such as silk provided the weight next, until the modern method of melting scraps from the manufacture of spin-casting monofilaments was perfected.

WHAT FLY LINE TO USE: Fly line is judged and measured by taper or shape. The most common tapers are:

✔ *L:* Level line with no taper but with memory of its previous life as a spin-casting line.

✔ *DT:* Double tapered line, which can be turned around if one end wears out and you hate to throw anything away. If cut in two, DT will make two lines, and if cut in three, is a starter kit for your brother-in-law.

✔ *WF:* A weight forward line, which allows more backing on the rod and a much longer cast due to a thinner belly line, reduces the need for the heavier lead sinkers to pull the lazy line off the reel. An exaggerated version called the shooting taper has a weighted head of at least thirty feet and can be used to knock small squirrels and wood ducks off low-hanging branches.

✔ *BBT:* A line with weight speed over twenty-five feet rather than thirty feet for fewer false casts which is good.

Fly line is also sold by the actual weight in grains (hectares in Canada) of the forward thirty feet.

Weight	Size
120 grains	#4
140 grains	#5
165 grains	#6
185 grains	#7
210 grains	#8
250 grains	#9

To match a line with a rod, the respective weights must be close to identical. For example, many lines are ninety feet. To cast two #4 lines in a #9 rod (twenty grains each), you'd need both spools of line rigged side by side and one large #10 lead sinker to total the necessary twenty-five grains (twenty-five degrees Centigrade without wind chill in Canada). Once that 180 feet of line is in the air, if it ever is, the ghost of Theodore Gordon will appear.

Here's another example. Say you wanted to load a #4 rod with #9 line. The line passing through the guides would look like your mother-in-law in spandex and you would have to throw it twice as hard or with both hands just to get the rope off the rod.

Buck doesn't need to tell you what floating (F) or sinking (S) line mean. The variations in S line depends on how fast you want it to sink: slow for a leisurely drift to the fish snoozing just below the surface, or fast to bury the metal spoon that will seriously agitate catch and release trout. An F/S designation means that the line has a sinking forward section. An AC/DC designation means it's time to change river guides.

Backing is the line that connects the reel spool with the fly line. Since the average length of fly line is about ninety feet, depending on who's giving good measure that day, order enough backing to reach the distant shore. The leader is what connects the fly line to the fly. All good leaders are tapered forward, the longer and thinner the better. The end of the leader attached to the line is called the butt and all fly-fishing purists have big butts. The end with a fly attached is called the tippet. The older, more childlike fly fishermen call this end Mr. Tippet.

LURES

Without making this section too long, it's important to admit to a few distinctions in the offerings fly fishermen make to their quarry (fish). Fly-fishing lures are not called bait, and the present-day method is to tie and "present" a lure or "fly" in exact imitation of the food the preferred species is attracted to.

At the risk of becoming too technical, saltwater fishermen catching the larger fish use larger flies. These flies will be called by the name of the fish they catch (like tarpon or striper fly) and many will be prefaced with the name of a famous fisherman designer. The telephone number of the artist is etched small under the feathers, should you have any questions on its use or want to demand a refund. Freshwater fishermen use a wider variety of flies as they have had more time to mull over things on the riverbank.

There is no popular template for indexing fly-fishing flies, and if there were, Buck wouldn't buy it. The common names of flies are generally left to precedent (yes, that is a Royal Coachman) or local custom (yes, your fly looks like a Royal Coachman, but around these parts we call it a Nonresident Royal Coachman and perhaps illegal in our pristine waters. Now, over here, is a nice selection of barely inexpensive locally tied flies for your review!).

✔ *THE DRY FLY:* This imitation stays on top of the water, floating on delicate feathers, or "hackles," like an insect. The hackles create a slight depression in the water which also distorts the image, so it's not too important to be exact. Hackles are created with feathers plucked from the necks of live barnyard chickens, with the premium colors coming from the necks of roosters. If you drive by a hackle farm early in the morning, you'll hear the sounds of rooster distress. A cock-a-doodle-doo indicates the groin feathers are being pulled. It's enough to wake up the whole farm. The pubic hair used in tying the sparse grey hackle fly is limited (and expensive) given the sparse number of graying flytyers.

BUCK'S BONUS TIP: If you need spousal hair to complete a fly, wait until he or she is asleep or passed out. Extra bonus tip: Back hair is much too curly for use on most flies.

When the materials themselves can't keep the dry fly's head above water, chemicals are added for waterproofing. These toxic chemicals won't pollute the waters if fished properly. Silicone or other waxy buildups to create buoyancy are called dressings. An English dry fly purist will wait for a hatch of insects to excite and make a trout "rise" and only then cast to the rising hatch. The more popular dry flies are the Wulffs, the Adams, the Light Cahill, and the Elk Hair Caddis. Latest research from Buck's Bait Shop and Entomology Laboratory has shown that fish are most attracted to the motion of the insect's sex life, and legions of Bucksters are busting chops with the following lures:

The Humping Humpy

The All Done Dun
(INSECTA COITUS FINISHICUS)

With wings laying flat postcoital hatchus interruptus, the All-Done Dun imitates a properly "spent" insect. These custom-tied flies may or may not be ordered from Buck via the publisher. A popular variation of the Humpy is the Happy Humpy Hooker, which has red booties and a shorter skirt. Other dry fly variations include wing positions that are straight up or curved for takeoffs, hackles that look like parachutes, and without hackles.

✔ *THE WET FLY:* Underdressed or almost-naked dry flies that are fished below the surface. The best of them tied to show no resistance to going down. Wet flies tend to be a little heavier than dry flies and can be used with weights to take the presentation right to the level of the fish. The more popular wet flies are the Blue Dun, the Muddler Minnow, the Royal Coachman, and the Dark Cahill. Wet flies have smaller hackles and wings similar in length to the body.

✔ *THE BUG:* A floating imitation with a body made from other materials such as cork, these bugs are the preferred flies for bass.

✔ *THE MIDGE:* An imitation too small to show in a book this size.

✔ *THE WOOLY BOOGER:* An adult nose easily holds three or four adult Wooly Boogers and the advantage of these lures is that you can leave them in place without a hook until you need them. Fly fishermen in the East blow them out into silk hankies while bass fishermen more conveniently shape then hook them while on their sleeves after a good sneeze. While it's not

The Wooly Booger

listed in the Encyclopedia of Southern Culture, there exists a native cult high up in the Ozarks, just past the last Foxfire exit, that crafts bass flies from butt hair. Folklore experts have identified these works of art as the original stink bait.

✔ *THE NYMPH:* Imitates the larval form of an insect that lives on the bottom of the stream until it swims or rises to the surface to molt and emerge as a winged dun flying to shore. The nymph is very small and very small gear is used for this technique.

✔ *THE STREAMER:* An artificial fly with either extra-long hair or feather wings that when wet imitates a small minnow. Buck tails are very durable streamer variations made from eyelashes from spotted fawns. Popular streamers are the Gray Ghost and imitations of most anything else found in favorite waters. Just south of the R. J. Reynolds ranch in western Wyoming, a popular fly is: The Marlboro Muddler:

Once used, there is little danger of secondary smoke.

The Marlboro Muddler

TECHNIQUES

Fly fishermen consider their sport not only a day of reflection but also a day of exercise. Golfers mouth a similar party line but with much uglier clothing. Fly fishermen golf in the summer when the streams are slow, but the two disciplines rarely mix since neither will listen to the other's mind-numbing stories.

WHAT YOU NEED TO KNOW TO FLY-FISH:

1. *READ THE WATER:* Discussed earlier in great depth and clarity. Okay to use reading glasses.

2. *PICK YOUR AMMUNITION:* To decide on the proper fly, buy a trout off a bait cranker and cut it open to see what they are eating. Buy, beg, or steal that imitation. Or scrape bugs off windshield.

3. *APPROACH THE WATER:* Sourdough McLean, fishing legend and artiste, is a stalker par excellence. Sourdough believes you can never start crawling or stalking too early. Crawling is the more natural means of locomotion and occurs naturally during childhood games that imitate military maneuvers or Indian treaty negotiations. Adult crawling coincides with last call at the

neighborhood tavern. Sourdough feels that this early morning crawl should not be interrupted by rascally habits like visiting an old girlfriend but, rather, continued right down to the river's edge. Unless the old girlfriend has her own teeth, he adds. When you've hit water, back-paddle several feet or until you are hidden by the tall grass. Then and only then, rest until daybreak. This will come quickly enough.

4. *CAST YOUR PEARLS:* In all likelihood, you have been to casting schools and practice your casting ad infinitum in your cul-de-sac. To fly-cast, you must first back cast to stretch out the line before it is to move forward.

The overhead cast is the basic fly fisherman cast. It is made up of the back cast, a dramatic pause for applause, and the fatal forward cast. Start with fifteen to twenty feet of line controlled with your left hand. Beginning at roughly ten o'clock, flip the line back to approximately two o'clock. Pause until the line tugs slightly, signaling that it's straightened out, then throw the line forward, stopping at ten o'clock again. If you continue on to, say, seven or eight o'clock, you are casting into supper time and it is time to quit. When the line is all the way out, gravity will kick in and pull your fly down to the surface. For longer casts, continue the motion while stripping out more line. That's it. That's all there is to it. Easy huh? And that's why fly fishermen use bigger words that most of us—it's all smoke and a means to keep us bait crankers out of their restricted waters.

The side cast and tower cast are just variations of the overhead cast to keep you out of overhanging trees and brush. The false cast is just that, moving a fly back and forth without it touching the water. The only other term and technique you need to know is how to mend your cast. When the current moves your line faster than your fly and interrupts its natural action, flip the middle or belly of the line upstream. That's it. That's all there is to it. Easy huh? Now you are free to mull on your own time and dime the mother of all fly-fishing muddles: presentation versus pattern.

Fly-fishermen prefer double-barreled shotguns to shoot fickle trout. Eastern fly fishermen prefer side-by-side 12 gauge shotguns with interchangeable chokes to harvest un-catchable and release fish, while Westerners favor over/unders in the more sporting 20 gauge. Full choke is used unless a school of trout needs your immediate attention.

BUCK'S BONUS TIP: **Most wet fly fishermen practice catch and release, but many purist dry flyers secretly imitate the Brit's use of a pannier to keep their catch. They prefer the large pannier that can be strapped to a donkey. The other dumb asses are further upstream.**

Purist fly fishermen kiss their first fish of the season on the mouth before release. It's impossible to underestimate the horror experienced by the fish in this action.

BUCK'S BONUS TIP: **Flyfishing "widows" are as easy to pick up as bass-fishing "widows." Mind you, wine is generally more expensive than draft beer.**

A
FISH
OUT OF
WATER

HOW TO DISPATCH A FISH

FOR THE TAXIDERMIST: Kill fish by clubbing between the eyes. If you hit the fish too hard, the eyes will cross, but a good taxidermist will straighten them. Wrap in a damp cloth and get to the studio as fast as you can. If you must freeze the fish, first wrap it in a damp cloth, and then put in a plastic bag. Ice cubes placed directly on the surface will discolor the skin and can't be used later in drinks. If you want to eat the fish after it's been skinned by the taxidermist, tell him. His personal freezer is probably full anyway. If you plan to mount your own fish, just skin and let it dry on something hard, like your wife's ironing board, and sew it shut, stuffed with old newspapers. Hang on wall.

FOR THE TABLE: Saltwater fish are often stuck and bled before being put on ice. Freshwater fish should be kept alive as close to the kitchen table as possible. Then kill the fish by clobbering it. The kids can clean the bathtub later.

With proper care, you've assured the family fresh, healthy fillets. Commercial fleets dump tons of fish in cool holds and let the combined weight and bouncing of the boat prepare the delicate flesh for fish sticks or

other food obscenities in the cannery. Smart market shoppers select long-line-caught fish, which are quick-frozen on the boats to stack better.

HOW TO CLEAN A FISH

Once you have caught the fish, the next task looms over every young fisher-man—what to do with the damned things. Fish can be buried somewhere, given to a neighbor who'll tell his wife he caught them, or cleaned as you're told to do. Not many Bucksters age their fish. British fly-fishing purists, however, hang their trout off the bumpers of their Land Rovers until the entrails fall out, claiming this "seasons" the meat properly.

The converted shed near the road at Buck's Bass Resort has a garbage pail, two scaling boards and scalers, a clogged drain, a leaky hose, and torn window screens through which gently wafting breezes carry whiffs of delight past the neighboring cathouses. Boat boys will clean your catch for fifty cents per pound so you can shuffle off towards the Valhalla Lounge with the others.

The only equipment you'll need is what Buck uses: an old six-inch Rapala flexible blade and a new, stiff seven-inch Uncle Henry knife. A plain dinner spoon can be used for scaling. If the fish has dried out, you either have one last opportunity to throw it away or can soak it in water for a few minutes. For a good grip, wet and salt your hands.

Trout are easy to clean. Cut from anus to gill junction and cut collar membrane free from jaw. With thumb and forefingers, pull backwards and you'll get it all. Use thumbnail to clean out black stuff along backbone. This is the fish kidneys, and if they are anything like yours, you'll want these out.

Most other fish are just as simple. Make a cut behind the head and pectoral fins to the backbone. Cut next to dorsal fin and forward along rib cage. Start pulling flesh back, and using a sharp knife, cut fish from rib cage to tail. Leave tail attached, flip over and repeat. Once flesh is off, lay fillet flat and with knife along skin side down, saw the skin from the fish to release great fillets.

For panfish, first scale the fish. Poke the sharp end of the knife into the bungus and cut shallow to the breastbone. With a finger, clean out guts and wash carefully. Cut off heads if you don't want the fish watching you eat.

Northerns are harder to clean. Have someone else clean them. Avoid belly or strong-tasting dark meat next to skin. No matter what the old timers tell you, the red spots on the bottom of the fish are not cheeks.

If your fish came from muddy water, skin first and then soak in a solution of two tablespoons of non-iodized salt and one teaspoon baking soda per gallon of water for twenty-four hours. Then wash clean. If your fish came from polluted waters, keep only the smaller, younger fish that haven't had time to absorb all of the toxins and give the rest to the neighbors.

Experts claim that if you both freeze and cook your fish properly, you will not have a problem serving fish. If you freeze your catch at minus 4 degrees Fahrenheit for seven days, most parasites will die. In Canada, leave the fish in the snow bank for 10 days or 120 kilometers, whichever comes first. Then cook until the fish flakes nicely and the translucency disappears, whatever translucency is (perhaps it's the soul of the fish, which would explain a few of the larger religious issues). See "fillet of sole" recipe.

HOW TO EAT FISH

It would be a fine kettle of fish is Buck didn't pass on his favorite fish recipes after all this work on how to catch them. Eat fish because it's good for you, not because you've heard it's brain food—evidence being the well-reasoned Vatican position on abortion. Every culture eats fish for a good reason. In the United States each person eats almost 16 pounds of fish and shellfish annually. This per capita figure is expected to rise substantially unless you are a Midwestern Catholic who already eats that weight in fish breading alone. Anglers eat up to 10 times as much fish as the typical American. Nutritionists have discovered that fish has more food value than Hostess cupcakes and that one 3.5-ounce serving of fish supplies about half the necessary daily protein. A half rack of good local beer will supply the rest. Fish is low in calories and in an effort to produce an even lower cholesterol fish, hatchery managers have introduced bran into their cornmeal fed mixture. In a 2-hour survey of 150 adult breeder salmon, serum cholesterol dropped up to 10 percent and each experienced firmer bowel movements.

There are only two major principles of fish cooking: how much fat the fish has and how to tell when it's done. Lean fish have less than 5 percent fat and include catfish, cod, halibut, perch, and snapper. The fat fish family includes salmon, trout, and tuna. The fat fish do not need any basting or sauces to cover the snag marks. An undercooked fish is translucent. Properly done, you can twist a fork into the fish and the milky white flesh flakes apart easily. The fish is over done when you can pick it up with a fork and comfortably hold it over the house cat.

HOME COOKING

The single most important reason why fish is not eaten more is that the fish stinks and the recipes are awful. Again, Buck comes to the rescue with tips and recipes designed to bring family and guests back into your kitchen.

Buy or better yet catch fresh (today's) fish. It's very hard to catch stinky fish, unless you are mooching feces-eating monster goldfish from New York City's sewers (see Flusher under "Freshwater Fish").

FISH BALLS FISKEBOLLER:
(FISK-A-BALL-AHR)

Only the largest trophy fish have external fish balls so you'll have to use this recipe for the small fish on your stringer. Mix 1 pound of firm white fish, 2 eggs, $1/2$ cup of cream and some flour in a food processor until smooth. Refrigerate while you raise the Norwegian flag on your poop deck. Bring a fish stock to boil. Use 2 spoons to form a ball and slide ball into boiling stock. If it falls apart, add more flour. Balls are done when they are firm. Much like Ole's blue balls after a week at sea. Strain the stock for use as a sauce base. Prepare a white sauce with the stock and some butter and flour. Serve with white boiled potatoes and any white vegetable on white bone china outside in a snowy white-out condition and you will have a Valhalla moment.

CHICKEN-FRIED FISH FILLETS:

Stir 1 beaten egg into 1 tablespoon milk and lay out 1 cup of finely crushed saltine crackers with salt and pepper to taste. Dip the fillets in the milky eggs first and then in the crumbs. Brown the fillets in a skillet of hot oil until done. It won't take long. See, there is no chicken in chicken frying. Another truth only found in this guidebook.

S.O.S OR CHIPPED FISH ON TOAST:

In a pan, cook 4 to 5 ounces of chipped smoked salmon ("squaw candy") in 2 tablespoons of butter for 3 minutes. Stir in 2 tablespoons flour and add 1 to $1/3$ cup of milk. Cook and keep stirring until thick and bubbly. Then cook a few minutes more. Add $1/2$ teaspoon Worcestershire sauce and pepper to taste. Serve on toast points. Serves two old lifer swabbies.

BUCK'S BONUS TIP: **The wood used for plank cooking salmon should be free of varnish and lead based paint, unless you prefer a nice glaze on the flesh.**

A method of low-impact fishing is to not forget the fish parts inside and in front of the more popular fillets. The great chef Escoffier discovered the tastiness of fish livers and would wash, dip in flour, and fry medium rare, adding pepper to taste. Since liver collects and stores much of the habitat abuse, use fish livers taken from waters you would drink. This limits you to the office cooler. Fish eggs can be cured into caviar or cooked according to a recipe collected by the late, great George Herter. Boil the eggs in water for six minutes, drain, and place in a bowl, adding an equal amount of cottage cheese and 1 level teaspoon of mustard for every cup of eggs you have. Mix all together until smooth and creamy, add salt and pepper to taste, and spread thickly on buttered bread. Fish tongues can be boiled in slightly salted water for about 10 minutes, drained, sliced, and served with Dijon mustard. See, more actual useful info!

OUTDOOR COOKING

NATIVE:

Wrap dry fish in birch bark and cover with tree sap overnight. Remove and let drip-dry. Grease griddle with bear or porcupine fat and fry on hot griddle skin-side down until done.

THE NEW AGE BOY SCOUT:

First apologize to the Girl Scout master for killing the fish. Following a short discourse on the soul of the trout taken, lightly sauté in the camp Calaphon skillet, being careful that no grease spills on your neatly pressed unisex scout cooking uniform. Microwave a packet of Lean Cuisine wild rice. Garnish with a sunflower. Serve with a carefully selected, chilled bottle of sparkling nonalcoholic wine.

While the New Age Scouts read Walt Whitman's *Leaves of Grass* around an electric log plugged into the scoutmaster's SUV, Coach edition, the evening breeze will just be able to carry the noises of the Buck's Jr. Bass Bastards camp downstream, sounds that are sure to include the opening of longnecks, pan-fried catfish, crackling, out of control fires, the smell of burned marshmallows and broken Hershey bars, the splashes of bare-butt swimming, and Buck's whiskey-soaked imitations of Robert Service.

 Buck's Bonus Tip: If you read *Leaves of Grass* backwards, you'll meet a serious recreational "user."

ETHNIC RECIPES

PEKING FISH:

A variation on this popular recipe is the Tiananmen Square Roast. Using any young fish fillet, crush the flesh using a bread roller with all your weight, breaking whatever small bones are remaining, sear the meat, and then act like nothing has happened.

LUTEFISK:

A chemically altered codfish, lutefisk (or lye fish) refers to fish that has been salted and dried. Originally skinned, boned, and soaked (or luted) in lye solution for 10 days, or however long it took big Ole to put his winter long johns on, and then rinsed for five to six days to "cure" the meat. A byproduct of wood ash, lye was originally used as a substitute for the more expensive salt. Too much lye and the fish get as mushy as Swedish meatballs. Too little, and the thicker parts aren't done.

Once in the kitchen, lutefisk is cooked by baking, boiling, or steaming. Wrapped in cheesecloth, the flesh is dropped in hot water, and then removed to steam dry and flake. Lutefisk is never cooked in an aluminum pot as it will turn the sensitive inner lining black, so you can imagine what it does to your stomach lining. Halfway through the cooking in very hot church kitchens, Finnish housewives come in to flog the chefs with pine boughs. In Lutheran churches all over the Midwest, lutefisk cooking is being taught to a whole new generation of apprentice chefs who have sworn to Buck on a plate of *lefse* that as soon as Dad starts "forgetting" the old times, they too will forget this vile national dish. Lutefisk will, however, continue to be served to seniors at the home who appreciate any soft meal.

Unlike most other Scandinavian foodstuffs, the good news about lutefisk is that it cannot be reheated (see Explosives).

CANNING FISH

Canning was discovered by Nicolas Appert to preserve rations for Napoleon's troops being sent away on maneuvers. Archeologists have found empty caviar cans along the route Napoleon used in his hasty retreat from Moscow in 1812 and first recorded the practice of littering freely and openly.

CANNED FISH:

Clean and ice the fish. Pressure-cook the fish to 240 degrees to kill *Staphylococcus aureus* and, more importantly, *Clostridim botulinum*. And any STDs from hatchery fish. Pressure cookers are large heavy pots with covers that can explode and kill innocent nonfishermen and have whistles that tell you when the cover will blow the cat out the door.

Brine is the solution that surrounds the fish when you pack it in jars. Mix 8 ounces of salt to 1 gallon of water and soak for 1 hour. If the fish is intended for a late-night movie-watching snack, use popcorn salt for flavor. For the less flavorful fish like pike and trout, add 4 ounces of salt. For bass, use at least 1 cup of salt; some cooks add a pinch of pepper.

If circumstances have reduced your supply but not demand for canned Omega-3 rich fish, take a look at what your cat is eating. You'll certainly find more appetizing items in the grocer's pet food section than what's found on your mother-in-law's table.

OTHER RECIPES

What with all the catch and release sanctions in place, it's almost impossible to bring home the evening meal without having a fit of ecological guilt. Old-timers learned that once the tourists left the riverbank, if all else fails, a quick snack was hiding in the bait box.

- *ANGLEWORMS:* Caution—do not bake in the microwave, as they will explode.
- *CRAWDAD:* Boil and serve with drawn butter. Whatever drawn butter is.
- *GRASSHOPPERS:* Dry-roasted, ground into a meal, or served whole in a stew. Locust-eaters panfry or barbecue a full skewer.
- *LEECHES:* If used in a blood sausage... the author can't continue. Sorry.
- *FROG:* If the bass haven't stripped off all the meat, skin, pull out the little guts, and bake.
- *MAGGOTS:* Survivalists warn against using maggots and grubs with hair as they may not taste as good as they look.
- *MINNOWS:* Game and fish officials do not want you to dump excess minnows in the water as it may introduce a species that will compete with the lazy resident game fish. Minnows can be prepared just like smelt, fried without cleaning.

OMEGA-3

Anthropologists excavating old, cold bones of Scandinavians and social scientists studying the life cycles of still-living Dutch fish eaters, have linked long life with concentrations of a marine fat called Omega-3. While both groups of scientists found both groups of subjects displaying the same amount of enthusiasm for the study, this fat has the ability to interfere with clot formation and is sought after by those with heart problems and major inflammatory diseases. Omega-3 is not a favorite of those with frequent bloody noses (like boxers or little brothers) or hemophiliacs. It's also contraindicated for women during their difficult days of the month, but then again, for most fishermen, they live long enough as it is. Fish oil helps fight malaria, some kinds of cancer, and, if the prairie dog research goes as expected, the inability to dig deep holes in the yard.

Studies show that consuming up to one gram per day of Omega-3 reduces by 40 percent the risk of death from coronary heart disease and cardiovascular disease in middle-aged American men. Two grams a day make most men rub noses with their women and, at certain times of the year, yearn to club baby seals. Omega-3 fatty acids are found in all fish—the fatter the fish the better—and are most concentrated in salmon. The only alternative to eating more fat fish is to eat pumpkin seeds in which case the diet should be accompanied by a good stool softener.

Watching the renewed American interest in fish as a health food, Norwegian fish farmers are tampering with gene pools to produce a new type of salmon with higher concentrations of this life-giving "fat," and the marketers are expected to introduce "fish lite" in several years. Norwegian fish biologists are also racing the clock to produce a thinner skinned fish that will keep the fish insides inside. It's hoped that this research would have human application, particularly among the Swedish fishing community. The Norwegian scientific community has almost abandoned efforts to reduce the large, square heads of Swedish farmed salmon but Lars says he'll have a final announcement before the next aurora borealis.

BUCK'S BONUS TIPS:

• Make sure you check your gal Friday for wood ticks on a regular basis. Ticks like your favorite spots, too.

• The American Fishing Tackle Manufacturers Association forbids catching fish with your own hands.

• Parcel post is the least expensive way to ship fish across country to your brother-in-law.

• Some resorts have a cast and blast program where you can shoot fish. Check with guides as to which firearms to bring.

• Wood oar handles can be rough and have splinters. Make sure your wife has a pair of good rowing gloves.

• Be careful in bear country. Tie the day's catch to the upwind pole on your mother-in-law's tent.

• Have your wife vary the boat speed while rowing. Erratic speed will cause your lure to act more like a live bait fish.

• A bar on a lake is a good place to fish. Not a bad place off the lake, either.

• Be thoughtful on opening day. A carpet remnant tacked to the bottom of the boat makes an ideal break area for your rowing wife.

• "Lute" in lutefisk means "Odin's soiled shorts" in Old Norwegian.

• Long eyelashes from spotted fawns make the best deer hair bass lures.

• Adding untreated stream water to your mother-in-law's whisky will prepare her for an early departure from the camp family reunion.

• Maggots will hatch if not refrigerated. Keep them in the little woman's yogurt.

• Petition your cable company to add Buck's *This Old Ice House*, a program bursting with tips on how to remodel your home away from the house.

THE LAW

RULES AND REGULATIONS

Fishing regulations are designed to distribute fish in a democratic manner, maintain large stocks of fish, and to prevent excess harvest of a species. Limits are set by concerned, caring public officials free from any political pressure. To manage the resource, they must first count all the fish with as many hands as are available, or trust honest sport fishermen to report his catch, or both, or none at all. Once the rules have been set, the regulations are published and distributed to the local bait shop reading rooms. Licenses are necessary to fish in most states.

TYPES OF LICENSES:

✔ *FOR RESIDENTS:* You have a choice of individual angler, senior angler, combo angler (with spouse or spouse equivalent, but she better not look like somebody's daughter), and a family of anglers license. Lifetime licenses are available for a lifetime of disappointment. If over forty, the license fees are higher since they wish to penalize those who can retire earlier than bureaucrats. If you move from that state, you have up to five years of visiting rights before they take your lifetime away.

✔ *FOR NONRESIDENTS:* In general, nonresident licenses are two to three times the cost of resident licenses. In a few southern states, you can marry a resident woman for a long weekend to get a free three-day pass, but only after all the local men have approved the match. In Maine, however, you are allowed to marry only old maids, defined roughly as when their looks start going, roughly around ten years old if living near the open water. Weekend grooms must swear not to lock the bride in the attic when discussing fishing strategy at the local brewery unless the attic has a window that faces the other direction and is swollen shut. No matter what nonresident license you buy, it's good for the length of time that it takes you to understand the big fish were caught yesterday by unemployed locals.

In addition to the licenses described above, nonresidents can buy more specific time on the lake with one-, three-, and seven-day licenses. Fishermen in a hurry can purchase an overnight or twenty-four-hour permit, and in the Northeast, inquiry licenses are required of those who insist on asking resident fishermen, "How are they biting?"

NEWS: A general fishing report for nonresidents from all fifty states: "You should have been here yesterday, last week, last year."

✔ *SPECIAL CONSIDERATIONS:* Generally speaking, you can fish free if you are a ward of the state, a patient in a state hospital, or sufficiently disabled to require a wheelchair, walker, or forearm crutches. If two or more of the above apply, the wardens are required to fish for you. The state can give free two-day licenses to the criminally insane but will not let them enter tournaments until they promise not to eat the bait or baiters. "Kids Free Weekends" are popular and allow resident adults to fish if supervised by children under the age of sixteen. Residents who are former employees of the U.S. Postal Service with at least one Christmas package–crushing award can fish at will and enjoy free franking privileges to mail the fillets home.

HOW TO BUY A FISHING LICENSE

If you are a nonresident, bring a large amount of tackle to the counter and, as they ask for your credit card and state driver's license, say you forgot the latter but know the other plastic will work. This tactic will work well even in fly shops if you display a calm, catch and release kind of demeanor.

If you are a resident, fishing licenses can be bought in places that fishermen most often frequent, such as Christian Science Reading Rooms, AA meeting halls, and the PTA. Wardens are authorized in most states to write licenses, and part of their employment contract requires them to stay up until midnight should an angler wish to stop by the house. In most cases, it's not even necessary to call ahead since the late hours are reserved for fish stories with the little woman while she patches his waders. The really friendly wardens will put out a little food for late-night visitors, and if the cupboard seems bare, it doesn't hurt to hint around for a snack. If the warden isn't home, his little woman has been deputized to perform all official functions, and if you have time for coffee, it's considered polite to listen to her woes of an absentee marriage. When she invites you to the back room to take license, you are receiving a major tax rebate.

VIOLATIONS

In most cases, violations involve the following infractions:

1. **You have no license at all.** The license must be carried with you on your person at all times. If you don't and a warden asks you to produce it, some states allow their officials to provide you an opportunity to find the misplaced license. In some states, it's appropriate to ask the officer to pick it up at your house, but only if the fishing is too good to leave right then. In other states, officer choices include coming in and having dinner with your wife while you are quietly bribing a tackle shop owner for a predated license or sleeping with your wife if you insist on illegally fishing at night.

2. **You have exceeded the bag limit.** In the good old days, bag sizes were the unofficial limits of the catch, and what you took home was limited only by the size of the gunnysacks. Now you are told exactly how many fish of a certain species you can have daily. For example, if the limit is fifty crappies, that's all you can catch and take home in one day. In some areas, however, two small crappies would seem to equal one big crappie and

with the language not being really clear, well, you know what I'm getting at. To settle issues of conscience like this, state fish and game departments have deputized nearby tavern owners and bartenders for the last word on the subject. The last word is normally offered as part of last call.

One common way to exceed your limit is to take one full limit, take that stringer home, and then go out to get another limit. Other common violations involve snagging game fish, taking too large or small a fish governed by slot length limits, and buying drinks for the few remaining attractive village women. All threatened fish species caught must be hand delivered to the warden's house and all endangered species should be eaten on the spot.

IF YOU ARE CAUGHT

Violators are usually taken to the lowest court of record such as a county or municipal court. In Canada, a Mountie on horseback can gavel a decision on his saddle horn and stash your bribe in his saddlebags. His husky, King, will act as sergeant at arms.

Most violations are misdemeanors of the fourth level and are subject to fines from nothing to 250 dollars with the possibility of thirty days in the hoosegow. Unlike game violations, most fishermen avoid license suspensions. Equipment used illegally in overbags is declared a public nuisance and confiscated in a civil suit. If your mother-in-law said, "go catch a lot of fish," she too will be taken unless they already know her down at the slammer as a public nuisance.

If you are caught in the Deep South doing usual Yankee mischief, when the warden says stand where you are, just drop your trousers so he can climb into the back of your waders for your penalty. If you squeal like a pig, you'll be able to go home early the very next day.

If you hire an attorney, a popular new defense plea is insanity due to multiple personalities, and your lawyer can claim that one of your more irresponsible personalities disregarded the law. In a countermove, state fish departments are enlarging the signature lines on licenses so each and every personality has an opportunity to sign in please.

In long conversations with judges and game wardens, Buck has learned that all rules and regulations would be dropped if fishermen just practiced simple etiquette such as:

- ✔ If you arrive at a fishing hole at the same time as another fisherman, yield to the angler coming from the right unless he/she is a nonresident, which automatically makes you right.
- ✔ If a newcomer is fishing a pool, generously go upstream to kick some fish down to him.
- ✔ In a drift boat, stay out of reach of shore fishermen casting treble-hooked spoons.

MISCELLANEOUS

COST OF FISHING

What is the true worth of a fish? Any kind of fish? Circuit judges and game wardens arbitrarily fix a value in very subjective terms. When but a little Buckster, a wily game warden snuck into Buck's basement to witness the cleaning of an improperly taken northern hiding among the spawning suckers. The fine was the cost of his spear (two dollars for the pole, ten dollars for the head) and a closed fishing season. In this case, the four-pound northern cost about three dollars a pound, but once you got all the bones out, it was probably more. But it also saved the expense of a whole season (worms, beer, firecrackers, French ticklers, etc) so who's to say.

Another way of looking at costs is to determine your real and imagined costs and divide those into what you bring home or, if you are a glutton for punishment, what is eaten. Fishing is touted as an inexpensive way to bring home the bacon. Let's take a look:

✔ Average mess of crappies: 3 pounds

✔ Average mess of crappie expense: $300

If broken down, it's easy to see why crappies are so costly:

> Minnows—$3
> Cuban Crooks cigars—$4
> Worms—$2
> French ticklers—$6
> Beer—$200
> Gasoline—$10
> Sun lotion—$4
> Beer nuts—$5
> Schmidt beer visor—$3

At first glance, the fish would cost 100 dollars a pound, probably more once you take off the scales, the bones, and give the fish heads to the Vietnamese

Relief Fund. But often you don't use all of what you take, except for the beer. You will have some lotion left over, a couple worms, a condom to wash out, and a bit of gas, so there is what accountants call a carry-over inventory.

MORE FREQUENTLY ASKED QUESTIONS ABOUT FISH AND FISHING

1. *How do Swedes jig for Northern Pike?*
   They lift their leg first, then their right leg, knees bent, then alternate.

2. *What's the difference between a nymph and a nymphet?*
   You take the former and I'll take the latter.

3. *You don't talk about catching shellfish, in particular crabs. How come?*
   As a non-resident rube, the local's crabs will catch you.

4. *How did "Max" end up with Sophia Loren in* Grumpy Old Men 2?
   His other nickname was "Stumpy".

5. *Are your whitey whites coming out as white as you'd like?*
   Yes, I swish 'em up and down in the new blue Cheer.

6. *Walleyes seem to bite better when it starts to get dark out. Will they bite as good if I just close my eyes.*
   He didn't want any of his people to feel like fish out of water.

7. *Do I have to take my clothes off to bear witness?*
   Yes, you do.

8. What's the brown stuff that squirts out of worms when you stick the hook in?

Philosphers call it the soul. Gourmands liken it to a brown sauce.

9. If a bear grabs your Alaska trophy salmon, can you shoot the bear?

Only if the fish is properly hooked.

10. If a guide grabs your Alaska trophy salmon, can you shoot the guide?

Only if you have an all-inclusive license.

11. I'm having premature ball closure during power casts with my new spinning reel. What do I do?

It's "bail" not ball closure, you nut case. Your crank is rank.

12. Is it more important to own a good fishing boat or to put food on the table?

It's much like the old chicken and egg question, or its modern equivalent— which came first, drinking or fishing?

13. Has fluoridation promoted healthier teeth in freshwater fish?

Surveys suggest that the fluoride found in toothpaste and dental rinses is an acceptable substitute.

14. If a rising tide floats all boats, what happens if you don't own a boat?

You're sunk.

15. Buck, you and your fishing buddies are barbarians. Your mother's eggs must have been addled.

I like mine over easy.

FISHING TOURNAMENTS

BIG SERIOUS ONES: Serious freshwater tournaments, orchestrated as the Superbowls of fishing, attract and create personality bass anglers and grand masters in a week of secret and not-so-secret fishing rituals. The final judging whips up a fever of media excitement and lure endorsements, and the trophy fish caught and released are also happy to be part of a larger world. The premier event revolves around smallmouths but mostly bigmouths prevail, if the Outdoor Channel is any indication. All freshwater tournaments follow general guidelines such as:

✔ *ELIGIBILITY:* Entrants must belong to the sponsoring or like society, be a practicing adult, and be free of tournament guilt. Applicants must have a valid fishing license or, if in a diminished capacity, a letter from their mother.

✔ *PRE-TOURNAMENT ACTIVITY:* Contestants must have all artificial habitat and fish traps in place by dusk the night preceding the tournament. Only non-lethal contaminants can be used in competitors' waters. Contestants may not visit competitor boats and steal their tackle or pitch woo to competitors' wives after the going has sounded. And having sex with a domestic pet before the tournament is a sin in Vermont.

 BUCK'S BONUS TIP: **Professionals use a slipknot when tying large bass to an undisclosed underwater location.**

✔ *TOURNAMENT ACTIVITY:* Each tournament has a fixed number of days, two or three days on average. Fishing partners are selected by the tourney judges without regard to race, color, creed, or history of farting, belching, and picking nose or butt hair. Entrants must fish only in tournament designated waters and cannot leave their boats unless an emergency thirst surfaces within sight of a flashing neon sign. All competitors must wear life vests unless she is a lady angler who has difficulty buttoning her life breast, er, life vest. In these cases, lady anglers are allowed to remove any constricting clothing unless it distracts potential competitors or current husbands. Fly fishermen won't notice. Use of alcohol other than that offered by senior tournament anglers is prohibited while fishing. An angler will be given a marking buoy that when placed in the water give exclusive rights to a seventy-five- to hundred-foot fishing circle. If that circle includes shoreline, a contestant can go ashore and relieve himself/herself. All others must hold it, which increases the fishing intensity.

✔ *EQUIPMENT:* Only legal baits and lures may be admitted. Contestants must identify their tournament rods to all within shouting distance, and no competitor can touch another's rod without permission. Contestant rods may be nicknamed and the tournament judges will rule on duplications. No radio communications outside the official tournament channels are allowed, but incoming cellular phone calls are allowed if from a competitor's wife.

✔ *WEIGH IN:* All fish will be weighed in and released to the fish probation officers. Fish release areas will be opened for general fishing to any disqualified pros from previous years. Officials reserve the right to conduct polygraph tests on bait fishermen. Fly fishermen are requiring sympathetic judges to probe for prostate problems at the same time.

 BUCK'S BONUS TIP: Load lead sinkers through the fish's mouth. The little red bunghole is too small.

✔ *SCORING:* Based on accumulated weight plus any bonus for perfect attendance, high score determines championships. In case of a tie, a fish-off or drink-off will settle who wears the crown. If the judges determine the best fishermen aren't photogenic enough for press releases, stand-ins are selected from the press pool.

The other tournament debate centers around the mortality of fish caught for inches, even though care is exercised in the catch, measurement, recording, and immediate release of these fish. Fish brought back in live wells to the big meat-hook scales for the Kodak photo opportunity have high mortality rates, particularly walleyes. Detractors say differences in water temperature, excessive handling, poor aeration in live wells, and then the final shame of losing the tournament for some swell bass fisherman is too much for an old fish heart to bear.

SMALL SERIOUS ONES: The International Game Fish Association (IGFA) is the official records keeper of all saltwater and freshwater fish. Catching record-breaking fish IGFA style requires a single angler to bait, hook, fight, and land a record fish without aid from others. An angler working a fish cannot be touched anywhere, especially in his most private areas, even by his woman.

Your fishing buddies who are always looking for a little on the side should have a pocketful of change for friendly wagers over the:

- *FIRST KEEPER*
- *FIRST LEGAL KEEPER*
- *LARGEST KEEPER*
- *FIRST ANY SPECIES*
- *SMALLEST KEEPER*
- *UGLIEST FISH*
- *UGLIEST WIFE*
- *MOST TOXIC FISH:* Like those finned time bombs lurking in marine waste dumps such as Commencement Bay in Tacoma, Washington, or the Boston harbor. Extra points are given for extra eyes and irregular fins.

THE FUTURE

Industry watchers note that the number of sport fishing participants shrink from time to time and blame the shrinking number of family farms, the break-down of the family unit, the increasing incidence of double incomes, the high cost of Starbuck lattes and the heartache of psoriasis. All the apologists overlook the two major concerns:

A REDEFINITION OF FREE TIME: In common parlance, free time is now called "quality time," and sitting idly on a lake waiting for something from under the water to do something is not perceived as the most productive way to use your quality time. If you must fish, it has to be complicated, expensive, and less codependent—like fly-fishing. Quality time has been reshaped into shopping at the mall, getting back to nature through the Discovery Channel, or worrying if you have the typical American family.

THE COMING INDOORS OF AMERICA: The average family has moved all members inside, in reaction to those rumors that the outdoors is nasty and brutish, while indoors is toasty warm and danger-free, particularly near the refrigerated snacks, the uncolas, and the teen cell line. Outside, you have to dress for the weather. Inside, you don't have to get out of your pajamas. Cold outside, warm inside. Bugs outside, none inside. Sunburns outside, sunlamps inside.

Fishing will be affected by trends that influence all aspects of society. The rate of population growth will slow as baby boomers approach middle age. Bass fishermen will continue to provide more than their share of children by marrying younger and prettier women than their first, second, or third wives.

America's population is growing older, and by 2025, the median age will be forty-one years old. What this means is that there will be more retired folks to take the new kids fishing if Dad can remember to bring the worms.

As you've suspected, minority populations in the United States are growing more quickly due to the immigration of third world Catholics and the general unavailability of condoms. By 2025, minorities are expected to make up about 35 percent of the population, and the other 65 percent will want to live elsewhere. Growth of fishing is expected from this minority explosion.

Non-family and smaller family households, the segment of the population that is increasing the fastest, are among the least likely to fish. It is simply impossible to take time to fish when you are in therapy.

Fishery managers are trying to encourage the growth of the sport and at the same time maintain the quality of the fishing experience. When less than half who fish buy licenses. Law enforcement officials are frantically trying to find the millions who did not buy licenses and will have better success once the GPS system is upgraded. Don't leave town!

AFTERWORD

Why fish anyway? Fish because you can fail at it! Fish because it really doesn't make any difference if you catch anything anyway. Fish... and take a kid with you.

Author Buck "Buck" Peterson pictured here in front of his fish shack after a day on Big Babe Lake deep in northern Minnesota lake country. The slab crappies will be donated to the Nordic Daughters of Olaf annual Mid-Summer Nude Frisky Frolic Festival. The saltwater species will be donated to the Son's of Big Ole Fish Fry on the other side of the lake. The walleye will be made into fish balls for Buck's regular patrons in the Valhalla Lounge. For pictures of the Frisky Frolic Festival, join Buck in his alternate universe at www.buckpeterson.com.